Breaking the Shackles

OF THE

DEMONIC

Deliverance, Healing, and Spiritual
Warfare for the Twenty-First Century

JUDITH L. GARCIA

BALBOA.
PRESS

A DIVISION OF HAY HOUSE

Balboa Press books may be ordered through booksellers or by contacting:

Balboa Press
A Division of Hay House
1663 Liberty Drive
Bloomington, IN 47403
www.balboapress.com
1 (877) 407-4847

Print information available on the last page.

ISBN: 978-1-9822-0483-9 (sc)
ISBN: 978-1-9822-0482-2 (hc)
ISBN: 978-1-9822-0484-6 (e)

Library of Congress Control Number: 2018906055

Balboa Press rev. date: 06/11/2018

Contents

Acknowledgments

I would like to give thanks to God for guiding me and directing me to write this book. I thank you for showing me the importance in this present time for people to understand about deliverance and spiritual warfare. I thank you, my Lord and Savior, Jesus Christ, for your sacrifice that you gave for me by dying on the cross that I could be saved and delivered and set free. I thank the Holy Spirit for his direction, teaching, and encouragement through every step of my life.

I would also like to give special thanks to my wonderful husband, William, who has been an inspiration to me in my Christian walk, spiritual warfare, and deliverance. He has always been right there beside me. He has always been a mighty man of God, full of insight and acting as a well of knowledge and encouragement.

Thank you to all of my deliverance team, who have stayed the course of time to help in advancing the kingdom of God. No words could ever express how grateful I am for these people and the sacrifice they have made for God's kingdom. Special thanks to Hector Santos, who reminded me every time I saw him to write this book. He showed me the importance of going forward and sharing this information to the body of Christ!

My Story

My story starts with meeting my husband. I was in my teens when we first crossed paths on my first job. I met him but never said more than hello and goodbye. I changed jobs two times after that, and I met him again. I didn't remember that we had met before. I didn't know Christ at this point of my life. I was partying and having what I thought was fun. I started to dabble in New Age, venturing into using potions and crystals. I got involved in horoscopes. I didn't think that it was witchcraft; I simply thought that it was make-believe and something fun to do. Bill kept trying to be my friend, but I thought that he was too arrogant, and so I ignored him.

A job came up that would be a promotion for me. It hadn't even been posted for the other workers to see. Bill heard about the job position and told my boss that he thought I would be perfect for the job. He told the boss that I was a serious worker, and he thought that I was smart and honest. The big boss called me into the office, told me that Bill had given me a reference, and said that he wanted to promote me into this position. I was shocked! I thought to myself, *why didn't Bill try to get the job himself? Maybe I was wrong about him after all.*

At the meeting with my boss, he told me that he wanted to send me to college at the company's expense. I couldn't believe my ears. I had never had the chance to go to college, and this was the chance of a lifetime for me. I said yes to the promotion. I would work during the day and go to college at night.

Months went by, and I didn't know it at the time, but Bill was telling all his friends that he was going to marry me.

Months later, I was working on my new job, and my boss wanted us to work together on some projects. This was how I got to know Bill as a friend. I had a new job, but everything else was slowly falling apart, and I could not figure out why. No matter how hard I tried, nothing was working out in my life. I kept telling Bill all the things that were going wrong, and he was always there to be a shoulder to lean on.

Years went by, and it only got worse for me. I was always depressed. I had many friends who had been killed in accidents at that time. My life now was spiraling out of control. One day after work, I was talking to Bill about everything I was going through. I called it bad luck. I told him that my luck was so bad that I didn't know what to do. He told me that he had the answer, that he could help me, and that he would get back to me. Well, he came back to me, and he had some things to give me. He told me that they would bring me good luck. He gave me a candle that I was to say a specific ritual over every night for a week, and he gave me oils and potions. I questioned Bill about whether this was witchcraft, and he told me that it was white witchcraft; it was not bad like black witchcraft. I believed him. I found out later that there was no difference between black and white witchcraft—it was all bad.

After the week that I burned the candles, applied the potions, and recited the curses, I got confused. I was scared and full of fear, and I still had all the problems on top of that! At that point, I was going to end it all. I called Bill to tell him that I couldn't take it anymore. Bill said to me, "Don't do it, Judy. Please just give me a chance to talk to you before you do anything crazy." He invited me over to talk, and he said that he'd met some very nice people, and they'd shared with him about Jesus Christ. He said that he'd been saved. He also said that he'd been delivered from witchcraft!

He told me that he could show it to me in the scriptures. As he looked and looked, turning the pages back and forth, his face started to turn red in embarrassment. He said, "Um, I know it is there, but I can't find it. But honestly, I am telling you there is scripture here that can help you." He said he'd been saved three days before, and so I knew he didn't know enough to help me. Then he told me about this Bible study that he went to, claiming that they would explain everything to me. Bill said, "These are very nice people, and I promise you that they can help you."

I went that night and was pleasantly surprised that they were very nice and friendly. We sat down at a table and talked. Little did I know that there were many people who were praying for me in other rooms and people at the table praying for me, breaking the curses that they knew Bill had placed over my life? The head of the Bible study shared with me all about Jesus Christ dying for my sins, saying that the Bible states we have to invite him into our hearts to be our Lord and savior, because he is a gentleman and will not force him on us against our own free will. She went on and on that night explaining everything about coming to Jesus, repenting of all of my sins, and the fact that this was a serious thing to not be taken lightly. It was about dedicating my life to the Lord.

I remember thinking to myself, *Okay, when is this lady going to stop talking? I want to get saved. I want this Jesus! This is what I have been looking for all of my life!*

Finally, she said, "Do you want to say the prayer of salvation?"

I quickly said, "Yes! I am ready." I felt such excitement and couldn't wait to do it. I said the salvation prayer, and as I was praying, it was hard to get the words out. While I said it, I saw the Lord standing in front of me with his arms open wide. It was real! I remember being so touched to know I actually saw Jesus Christ, and I cried and cried. They had me repent of all works of darkness, and after that I renounced all curses I had over my life. There was quite deliverance, and that night as I went home, I remember that everything in my life felt so different. I was no longer depressed. Everything looked so different. I was so thankful that I'd had a chance to meet these people. This was the beginning of a huge change in my life!

A lot of things got broken that night, but not everything. Although Bill went through two days of deliverance and many things were broken, he still had a ways to go too. Right after that, Bill said to me that he had deceived me on purpose to get me involved in witchcraft. He apologized to me and said he wouldn't blame me if I never spoke to him again. I forgave him, and I saw the sincerity in him as a person: he had a huge heart to come to me and to ask for forgiveness. Bill went to every person whom he'd involved in witchcraft. He apologized, told them about Jesus Christ, and tried to lead them to the Lord! Some got saved and some didn't want to hear it, but at least they were told the truth. Bill was set to become high priest in witchcraft when God intervened and stopped the plan of the devil! God orchestrated so many things all at the same time to bring us both to him, to the point of bringing us forty-five minutes away from where we lived to attend a powerful Bible study. But it was much more than that—it was a deliverance ministry. They knew what they were doing, and they knew what it was going to take to get us straightened out.

Months went by. We went to church on Sundays, and we went to Bible studies and to care and share groups. We learned about the Lord and got stronger in him! We were so hungry to know all that we could know about God and to get closer to him. It was wonderful. One day Bill heard a word from the Lord, and the Lord told him that he wanted Bill to marry me. Bill proposed to me, and we were married shortly after that.

It was a long road from there because we had prophets from all over telling us that we were going to have a ministry that would snatch souls from the pit of hell. We would visit churches, and the pastors would stop in the middle of their messages and tell us that they saw visions of souls being saved from the pits of hell. They claimed that we had a very strong ministry of deliverance. This was where it all started. We had a lot to learn, and the attacks we went through in our early years were great. The devil was angry that we were both set free and using our newfound freedom for the kingdom of God. We learned that we had to stand strong and learn all that we could learn, and that we would pull through the difficulties with God by our side if we stayed faithful.

When we first came to the Lord, pastors and prophets spoke over us about the vision for our ministry that we would have a very powerful spiritual warfare and deliverance ministry. We started a Bible study, and at that time people started coming to us who needed deliverance. They came from all over. We were not looking to do deliverance at that time and were concerned only about the Bible studies, but it seemed that God had other ideas. Many times people would come, and we would think, *how did this person even find us?* But God did what he had to do to get these people set free. Then we started our own ministry, where God brought to us many who needed healing or deliverance. Some churches started sending us people to have them set free or to receive healing. The information that we learned from the dark side, we now used for God's glory!

Through the years, I have seen thousands of people who are desperate to be set free from the occult. It seems that more people are getting involved in it than ever before. They are promised power by the enemy, but many times their lives turn to sorrow, depression, gloom, and despair.

While I was in the process of writing this book, my husband suddenly passed away. He had not been sick that I noticed, so this was unexpected. But the Lord said to me that the vision had not stopped. He told me that it had only just begun. I was surprised by what I heard. The Lord reminded me of a conversation that I'd had with my husband, where my husband gave to me the deliverance ministry and said, "I give to you everything." My husband did not want to do deliverance anymore. I told my husband that this was his gifting and calling. My husband said, "Well, I am giving this to you." The Lord told me that he gave you the mantle of the ministry. The Lord said to me, Bill gave you the whole vision of this ministry. He handed it over to you. The Lord then said to me, for the vision to come to pass, you have to step into alignment with what I have given to you, and carry on the vision. The vision God has given to me for the future of Risen Savior Christian Center will be a teaching and learning center for spiritual warfare, deliverance, healing and miracles. I heard the Lord say, "This is going to be much bigger than you, much bigger than your church, and even much bigger than Rochester, New York." He then said that this would touch America and beyond. The Lord said he would be bringing seasoned intercessors to my side to be a huge prayer army, as well as those gifted in deliverance to be able to handle the huge outpouring of people who will need deliverance in these days to come. When he spoke to me, he called this center a command center from heaven to tear down the devil's kingdom.

Effective Prayer

If my people which are called by my name will humble themselves, and pray, and seek my face, and turn from their wicked ways; then will I hear from heaven, and will forgive their sin, and will heal their land.
—2 Chronicles 7:14

I cannot emphasize enough the importance of prayer to a believer. In these days in America, we are seeing more evil becoming more commonplace in every area of the country. We are seeing shootings in the schools. The evil is more frequent and on a larger scale than we could have ever believed. We are hearing of policemen being shot and killed in our streets while sitting in their cars. When I was a young girl, if I heard of someone getting killed, it was very unusual. Now it seems to have become commonplace. Shootings are happening in movie theaters, in shopping malls, at gas stations, and on the streets while people are taking walks at night.

We see people openly professing to be into witchcraft, Satanism, and New Age. We see psychics proclaiming to us on television and on the Internet to call their hot lines, and they will tell us our future. I went to a restaurant one night with my husband and my nephew. We went to a restaurant that we used to go to all the time, but this night something felt very different. I felt uncomfortable and didn't know why, but I didn't say anything. I sat down and opened the menu to order my food, and my husband said to me, "Honey, look around you. I asked him why, and he replied, "Just trust me. Look behind you!"

I did, but I didn't notice anything. I didn't want to be rude by staring at people, so I said, "Honey, I don't know what you are talking about." He said over and over to look at the people who were around us. I looked again, noticed a person reading a Bible, and said, "Oh, how nice."

My husband quickly said, "No, that is not the Christian Bible—that is a Satanic Bible." I looked around and noticed something very strange. Everyone was wearing black—black clothing, black jackets, and black makeup on the ladies. The next thing I noticed was a man with a picture of Satan on the back of his jacket. Then I noticed long, black fingernails on the women. My husband overheard some of the people talking about their course they were taking in college in witchcraft, which was required by the college.

At that time, my husband turned to me and said, "We are sitting right in the middle of a witchcraft club!"

After my husband said this to me, our waitress came to take our order. I will never forget the stress on her face when she asked us if we were ready to order. She shared that she was so confused she could hardly write down our order. She explained that since these kids had started coming to the restaurant, she couldn't think clearly and was having severe headaches. She was upset and said, "I can't even think."

I began to pray. "Lord, what do you want me to do? How do you want me to deal with this?"

The Lord clearly told me to anoint this place. He told me where to anoint. He told me to get up go to the bathroom and start there. Then he said to come back and anoint under our table. He told me that he wanted it anointed with oil in places that would not be easily washed off, and so I did. He told me to start breaking the curses and spells of witchcraft.

When I finished and looked up, everyone was gone. They left so fast that I couldn't believe my eyes. But my job was not over. I knew that God wanted to penetrate this cult group, and so every day I prayed for these kids and all of the kids in my city, praying for God to be revealed to them. I prayed for their curses to be broken, and I prayed for God to saturate them with his truths and break the deceptions in of their lives. I felt a strong feeling to pray for that waitress. I broke the curses of confusion on her, and I broke the curses of witchcraft.

A month later, this restaurant was shut down, and it never ever reopened. That was years ago, but I never forgot what happened. I became fully aware of how much witchcraft had entered our culture. It was growing and becoming a part of our everyday lives. But that first time, I looked and didn't notice anything wrong. I realize now that it was because I would never have suspected it to this degree. Therefore I was not looking for witchcraft in the public arena to this degree, just out in the open. They weren't hiding it at all! It wasn't until I looked again and again at what was going on that I noticed it. All through this situation, I continued to pray to God for direction. I asked him to show me what to do and how to deal with it. We can never underestimate the power of prayer. If I didn't seek the Lord in this matter, I wouldn't have known how to handle it in an effective way.

Months later, one of the girls from this group came to us and accepted Jesus Christ as her Lord and Savior. This girl continued to get ministered to, and she was set free from the occult. She has been with our ministry now for years and is a very strong person in our church. What she used for the devil, she now uses her gifting for the kingdom of God, bringing souls to Jesus Christ.

> The effectual fervent prayer of a righteous man availeth
> much. (James 5:16)

Effectual implies to me that there can be an effective or ineffective prayer. The effective prayer is the prayer that we do after we seek God's wisdom and guidance.

> I exhort therefore, that, first of all, supplications, prayers, intercessions and giving of thanks be made for all men: For kings, and for all that are in authority; that we may lead a quiet and peaceable life, in all godliness and honesty. (1 Timothy 2:1–2)

> Who will have all men to be saved, and to come unto the knowledge of the truth. (1 Timothy 2:4)

This implies that God wants us to have precise knowledge and correct knowledge. When we pray about deliverance, we need to have precise knowledge and correct knowledge. Prayer is not just a vehicle that we use to pray out what we think or what we see. It is the vehicle to pray out what God thinks and knows that is hidden or unseen to the naked eye. He sees all things. We may see something that is evil, but God knows what is at the root cause of that evil. What spirit is driving that evil? What door did this person leave open in his life, through sin or through tragedy that left an open gateway?

We can call on the Holy Spirit, who searches the deep things of God for our lives. We can ask for the Holy Spirit's revelation into a situation to clearly show us how to pray to push away and destroy the darkness in a life, in a city, in a state, or in our country.

Since taking prayer out of schools, the attack on the Ten Commandments being displayed in our courts, and our crosses being ordered taken down, we can clearly see more and more evil in America.

> This know also, that in the last days perilous times
> shall come. For men shall be lovers of their own selves,
> covetous, boasters, proud, blasphemers, disobedient to
> parents, unthankful, unholy, without natural affection,
> trucebreakers, false accusers, incontinent, fierce,
> despisers of those that are good, traitors, heady, high
> minded, lovers of pleasures more than lovers of God.
> (2 Timothy 3:1–4)

We are seeing this in our society on a daily basis now, and I do think that we are living in the last days. We see school shootings. We see our policemen being shot and killed. We see more and more drugs on the streets, with people being shot over drugs. We hear of wars and threats of war. We hear it on the news on a more frequent basis every year. The Bible warns us that in the last days, perilous times will come. We need to be about the Father's business, praying in an effective way to push back the darkness and to cause all men to come to the knowledge of truth! Without effective and fervent prayer, we will not see deliverance from evil spirits and deliverance for the areas in which we live.

> For we wrestle not against flesh and blood, but against
> principalities, against powers, against the rulers of the
> darkness of this world, against spiritual wickedness in
> high places. (Ephesians 6:12)

Just like there are different ranks in our military, there are different ranks of demons in the spiritual realm controlling different people, places, and situations! The spiritual realm is very real! There is the kingdom of God and of the light, but there is also a very real realm of Satan and of the darkness. We have been given the power through prayer to overcome the devil's kingdom. As Jesus cast out spirits, the blind were able to see, and the deaf could hear. What will we be able to do through the power of Jesus Christ our Lord? The precious blood of Jesus Christ that he shed on the cross gave us access to cast out spirits, break curses and spells, and heal those who are oppressed by spirits, demons, principalities, powers, and rulers of darkness.

We cannot ignore the spiritual realm in the hopes that it will go away on its own. Spirits of darkness do not go away simply because we ignore them. Jesus is our example in all things that we face in life. When Jesus was led up into the mountain to be tempted by the devil, he used the Word, the light of the truth of God, to counteract the lies of the devil and expel him.

> Then was Jesus led up of the Spirit into the wilderness to be tempted of the devil. And when he had fasted forty days and forty nights, he was afterward an hungred. And when the tempter came to him, he said, if you be the Son of God, command these stones to be made bread. But he answered and said, It is written, Man shall not live by bread alone, but by every word that proceedeth out the mouth of God. Then the devil taketh him up into the holy city, and setteth him on a pinnacle of the temple, and saith unto him, If thou be the Son of God, cast thyself down: for it is written, He shall give his angels charge concerning thee: and in their hands they shall bear thee up, lest at any time thou dash thy foot against a stone. Jesus said it is written again, Thou shalt not tempt the Lord thy God. Again, the devil taketh him up unto an exceedingly high mountain, and sheweth him all the kingdoms of the world, and the glory of them: And saith unto him, all these things will I give thee, if thou wilt fall down and worship me. Then saith Jesus unto him, get thee hence, Satan: for it is written, Thou shalt worship the Lord thy God, and in him only shalt thou serve. (Matthew 4:1–10)

> And when the devil had ended all the temptation, he departed from him for a season. (Luke 4:13 KJV)

> And when the devil had finished every temptation, he left him until an opportune time. (Luke 4:13 NKJV)

> When the devil had finished tempting Jesus, he left him until the next opportunity came. (Luke 4:13 NLT)

This scripture first tells me that there is a war, and that even the demons were warring against Jesus Christ himself. The demons tried to trick him, and when they were defeated, they looked for a more opportune time to strike him. We know by this scripture that the devil never really takes a vacation. He is looking for a better opportunity to hit the believers. Satan hit Jesus when Jesus was weakness. He had been without food and water and was in a weakened state. But Jesus defeated him. The Bible states that Satan departed for a season. Satan is looking for the times of weakness in our lives, or a time when we are not expecting the attack. We need the Lord at all times. We need to be prepared before the attack comes.

> Behold, I send you forth as sheep in the midst of wolves: be ye therefore wise as serpents, and harmless as doves. (Matthew 10:16)

We need to be as wise as serpents but as harmless as doves, because the demon spirit realm is real. I am not giving glory to the devil, but Jesus himself said that the serpents are wise. They are wise only in trickery and deceit.

Gone are the days that we can ignore the darkness around us, and we think those who are doing witchcraft, sorcery, spiritism, divination, and voodoo will never affect our lives. However, they are all around us, and have permeated our society in every area. The Church needs to arise and do the works that Jesus did. The Church has to become strong in these last days against spiritual darkness. In my heart, I feel that more and more, we will see people crying out to be delivered, and they need the help of those who know how to deliver them from the demonic realm.

> If my people who are called by my name will humble themselves and pray. (2 Chronicles 7:14)

Prayer is a powerful tool that needs to be used as much as possible! We Christians cannot afford to take a vacation from the warfare God has called us to do.

I know from my former life in witchcraft, and what my husband was involved in, that the devil's people are praying continually! They take it seriously. However, they do not have the power though that we have. God's people need to know that they have the ultimate power through God, which supersedes the devil's power. Christian believers do not have to be in fear when they pray, knowing that all of heaven is backing them in their prayers.

Jesus said to Peter in Matthew 16:19, "And I will give unto thee the keys of the Kingdom of heaven." We have also been given the keys to the kingdom, and one of them is prayer. We are commanded to be instant in season and out of season (2 Timothy 4:2). This tells me that as believers, we need to be prepared at all times and know what to do in an instant through prayer and seeking God.

> Ask, and it shall be given you; seek, and ye shall find; knock, and it shall be opened unto you: For every one that asketh receiveth; and he that seeketh findeth; and to him that knocketh it shall be opened. (Matthew 7:7–8)

To be prepared for effective deliverance and spiritual warfare, we need to be in the attitude of prayer, always asking, seeking, and knocking on the door of God's heart for his insight and wisdom. I ask the Lord to give me wisdom and knowledge for anything that is coming my way, and I pray for God to direct my footsteps.

One day we went shopping, and as we were returning home, we went by a field that was in front of a forest of trees. As we drove by, I noticed limousines that were driving into that forest, and I remember thinking that was very odd because it was a rainy day. I noticed the people getting out of the limousines, and at first I thought, *Oh, how nice. Someone has been married, and they are out taking pictures.*

But then I noticed a huge pot, and all the people were in black, including the bride. I felt very strongly to tell my husband that we needed to stop the car and back up. I explained to my husband what I saw, and he was concerned as well. We backed up the car and watched. I then prayed to God to ask him, "Why are we at this particular place and time to see this and what do you want us to do?" I knew that this was more than a coincidence. It seemed that many times we were at the right place and the right time to see something that God wants us to pray about. My husband and I knew that this was a satanic ceremony, and most likely there could be a blood sacrifice. We stayed and prayed, and we broke the curses over this ceremony. We also prayed for the plans of Satan to be frustrated, and that the angels of God would be sent forth to stop this ceremony and stop these people from harming anything or anyone. We waited and prayed until the ceremony stopped. We felt that our prayers were answered, and we both had a good feeling inside of us that everything was okay at that point, so we left. All glory to God!

This is just one instance of a situation stopped because of people praying while directed by God, believing and standing in faith to pray against something that was evil and to change the outcome. I believe that all Christians have that power through prayer to change the atmosphere

9

and stop the demonic activity through the name of Jesus and through the blood of Jesus Christ, if they believe that all things are possible through God.

For example, if we see in our city a specific sin that is being done, like porn shops or strip clubs, the curse placed on that area could be lust, sexual perversion, worldliness, manipulation, and control. We have the power to bind up these curses and break them in the name of Jesus. Then we can break the spirit of whatever curse that God has revealed to us. If it was a curse of perversion, then we could also break the spirits of perversion over that area. If it is a curse of murder in that area, we can break the curse that is allowing the spirits to come into that area, and then we bind up the spirits of murder in that area.

There can be other spirits, such as destruction, hatred, and anger. All of these spirits could have the same assignment in the end, as a spirit of murder or curse of murder, or they could be working together with that spirit of murder to accomplish that same assignment of darkness. I call these lookalike spirits. They have a different name but have the same assignment. Curses of anger over an area or person can cause people to get so angry that they murder someone. The curse of anger or rage, and the spirits of anger and rage, can be a problem over an area and can cause murder.

This is just one example of many things that can occur over your area. It is very important to pray to God for his knowledge and wisdom in revealing the curses and demonic activity that have to be broken in your area.

Strategies and Tactics

Over the past few years, I've watched generals and commanders talking about war on the news, specifically about the war in the Middle East. I noticed one thing that they say over and over about how they were supposed to handle a war, and that was they had to have a strategy to win the war. You have to wage the war to win. The second thing to winning a war that I heard from their mouths is that you have to understand your enemy in order to be successful. You have to name your enemy. You have to know who your enemy is. You have to know his strategies, and you have to know his mind-set to beat him! How can you stop your enemy if you do not know what he will throw at you? I also noticed something that was said, and that was that the soldiers in Iraq were throwing down their weapons and running; they weren't prepared to fight.

I knew that God was showing me one of his nuggets of truths. The war waged by our military is very similar to the war we fight against the devil's kingdom. God gives us very real strategies to defeating the devil. To win, you have to know your enemy, what his tactics are, and what he is about so that you know how to defeat him. We cannot throw down the weapons of our warfare and run. We must stand and fight the good fight of faith.

> For though we walk in the flesh, we do not war after the flesh: For the weapons of our warfare are not carnal, but mighty through God to the pulling down

of strongholds; Casting down imaginations, and every
high thing that exalts itself against the knowledge of
God, and bringing into captivity every thought to the
obedience of Christ. (2 Corinthians 10:3–5)

Paul is explaining in this passage that there is a warfare to be done by
the believer. Our warfare is mighty and powerful because it is through
God, and we can pull down strongholds of the devil that have people
bound up and oppressed and weighed down. Every evil imaginable can
be brought under the obedience of Jesus Christ. Evil demons exalt
themselves against the good thoughts that come from heaven, but we
can bring them to subjection by the name of Jesus and through the
blood of Jesus Christ!

Thou therefore endure hardness, as a soldier of Jesus
Christ. No man that warreth entangleth himself with
the affairs of this life; that he may please him who has
chosen him to be a soldier. (2 Timothy 2:3–4)

This scripture tells me that we are all called to be soldiers of the Lord!
What does a soldier in the natural world do? He strategizes, he analyzes,
he protects, he fights, and he lays down his life, if necessary, to win the
war against his adversary!

We are called as soldiers of the Lord, called into the army of God! We
are meant to occupy and take over the devil's kingdom for God.

And he called his ten servants, and delivered them ten
pounds, and said unto them, Occupy till I come. (Luke
19:13)

This was Jesus speaking to his followers, to occupy till he comes. We
first have to know that there is a war to win. When you came to Christ
and asked him into your heart as your Lord and Savior, you enlisted

into his army! But our army consists of God the Father, Jesus the Son of the Living God, the Holy Spirit, and innumerable angels.

> And from the days of John the Baptist until now the kingdom of heaven suffereth violence, and the violent take it by force. (Matthew 11:12)

In the *Vines Expository Dictionary*, the word *violent* is translated as *biazo*, which means to antagonize. And "the violent taking it by force" is translated as *biastes*, which means a forceful man. This means that we are to be forceful in spiritual warfare against principalities and powers, as well as the rulers of darkness. This does not mean that we are cruel; on the contrary, we are supposed to be loving. But we can take everything up in prayer. We can change things for the good. We don't have to tolerate the antagonism of the devil. That is really whom we are fighting.

Jesus gave us all power against the devil. Amen!

Now that we know that we are in an army and are fighting a war for Christ, we have to know what strategies Jesus gave us in the Word.

When he goes into battle, a soldier has to dress in his combat uniform, which is designed to protect him. The military has camouflage colors to blend into the surroundings and not be seen by enemies. Soldiers have helmets to protect their heads, from the blast of bombs. They have a strong material that makes up the uniform that will not be torn up in case they have to go through water, heavy brush, or desert. The boots won't wear out and will be tough enough to protect the soldiers' feet.

Our uniform is the whole armor of God, and it is tough in protecting the Christian soldier. It covers the whole body. But our clothing is spiritual, and this clothing from God is designed to protect us. It is tough and is given to us by God the Father to protect us from anything that the devil and his army can throw at us.

The Whole Armor of God

One strategy that the Lord gives us is to be dressed with the whole armor of God.

> Finally, my brethren be strong in the Lord, and in the power of his might. Put on the whole armor of God, that ye may be able to stand against the wiles of the devil. For we wrestle not against flesh and blood, but against principalities, against powers, against the rulers of the darkness of this world, against spiritual wickedness in high places. Wherefore take unto you the whole armor of God that ye may be able to withstand in the evil day, and having done all, to stand. Stand therefore, having your loins girt about with truth, and having on that breastplate of righteousness, And your feet shod with the preparation of the gospel of peace; Above all, taking the shield of faith, wherewith ye shall be able to quench all the fiery darts of the wicked, and take the helmet of salvation, and the sword of the Spirit, which is the Word of God. (Ephesians 6:10–17)

We cannot go into battle for our fellow brothers and sisters in the faith; for our churches, towns, and cities; or for our nation without being dressed for the battle. Certainly we cannot go into deliverance to set someone free from the demonic chains without being dressed for the battle. The whole armor of God is the battle clothing for us to fight! We are dressing ourselves with God's holy discernment and holy protection for every part of our being.

Every day, I picture myself putting on this armor before I go into my day. This armor is the protection of God over my life. The Word of God says to put it on, and I take this word literally. In verse 17, it says that we can stand against the wiles of the devil. In the *Vines Expository Dictionary*, *wiles* is translated as *methodia*, which means craft, deceit, a cunning device, or a lying in wait. The devil is lying in wait to deceive, and he is cunning and crafty. But we have the armor of God and the Word of God, which will protect us and expose the lies of the devil for what they are. If we want victory in our lives, we must put on the whole armor of God!

The helmet of salvation constantly reminds us that it is by the love of God that we are saved—that is, by the death and resurrection of God's only son, who went to the cross for us. Jesus shed his blood on the cross for us to wipe away our sins and cleanse us from all unrighteousness. The helmet of salvation is there to constantly remind us that we are saved if we name the Lord Jesus as our Lord and Savior and ask him into our hearts. The devil cannot lie to us and tell us that we are not saved! Romans 10:9 tells us this helmet of salvation stops the condemnation of the devil when he would like to tell us that we are no good and cannot be children of God because we have sinned too much, or when he brings up our past to embarrass us. The helmet will cause you to receive from God that you are a child of the Most High, and that his blood bought you and is able to uphold you, making you worthy because of the finished work of the cross.

The breastplate of righteousness

The blood of Jesus Christ makes us righteous and cleanses us from all of our sins. God sees us through the blood of his son.

> If we confess our sins, he is faithful and just to forgive
> us our sins, and to cleanse us from all unrighteousness.
> (1 John 1:9)

When we repent of our sins, God forgives us and remembers that sin no more. It is the devil who will constantly try to remind us of what we have done wrong in the past. When the devil says that we are not good enough and reminds us of all of our sins, the breastplate of righteousness, which is from God, is there to remind us that we are good enough not because of anything we have done but because God made us righteous through Jesus Christ who has forgiven us, cleanses us from all unrighteousness, and remembers our sins no more!

> And hereby we know that we are of the truth, and shall
> assure our hearts before him. For if our hearts condemn
> us, God is greater than our heart, and knoweth all
> things. Beloved, if our hearts condemn us not, then
> have we confidence toward God. (1 John 3:19–21)

One of the tricks of the devil is to tell us that we are not worthy, and to bring condemnation to the body of Christ. God's Word says that there is no condemnation to they who are in Christ Jesus and who walk not after the flesh but after the Spirit.

The Belt of Truth

When the devil tries to lie to us, the belt of truth saturates us with God's truth to counteract the lies that Satan speaks into our minds or through others. The enemy tries to pull us away from God's plan for our lives through his lies. Nowadays, there are many doctrines floating around, and if God's people are not filled with the Word of God and covering themselves in the armor and through prayer, they might not be able to know what is the real truth and what is the deception. We need God's truth to cover us in everything that we do.

We are of God: he that knoweth God heareth us; he that is not of God heareth not us. Hereby know ye the spirit of truth, and the spirit of error. God wants us to be filled with His truth that comes from His Holy Spirit. (1 John 4:6)

Now the Spirit speaketh expressly, that in the latter times some shall depart from the faith, giving heed to seducing spirits, and doctrines of devils; Speaking lies in hypocrisy; having their conscience seared with a hot iron. (1 Timothy 4:1–2)

There are doctrines of the devil that can seduce people away from the truth, and that comes from the lies demons speak into their heads. Some of the lies he speaks into Christians minds are that they are not good enough, they were never saved, they can worship God at home, and this walk is too hard. There are too many to list them all.

However, we have God to always fill us with his truths if we ask him. He wants all of his children to have his wisdom and knowledge. I always say that if it doesn't up build, edify, or encourage, then it is most likely not from God. Even God's correction edifies and builds up!

The Sword of the Spirit

The sword of the spirit is the Word of God.

Then was Jesus led up unto the wilderness to be tempted by the devil. And when he had fasted forty days and forty nights he was afterward an hungered. And when the tempter came to him, he said, if thou be the Son of God, command that these stones be made bread. But he answered and said, It is written, Man shall not live by bread alone, but by every word that proceedeth out of the mouth of God. Then the devil tooketh him up into the holy city, and setteth him on a pinnacle of the temple. And saith unto him, If thou be the Son of God cast thyself down: for it is written, He shall give his angels charge concerning thee: and in their hands they shall bear thee up, lest at any time thou dash thy foot against a stone. Jesus said unto him it is written again, Thou shall not tempt the Lord thy God. Again, the devil tooketh him up into an exceeding high mountain, and sheweth him all the kingdoms of the world, and the glory of them; And saith unto him, all these things I will give thee, if thou wilt fall down and worship me. Then saith Jesus unto him, Get thee hence, Satan: for it is written, Thou shalt worship the Lord thy God, and him only shalt thou serve. Then the devil leaveth him, and, behold, angels came and ministered unto him. Three times the devil tempts Jesus but Jesus uses the word of God to defeat the devil. Saying each time it is written! This part of the armor will help us in skillfully using sword of the Spirit, which is the Word of God. The Spirit is the Holy Spirit, who will be there for us to bring to us just that right scripture as we need it, as we wield that sword against the devil! (Matthew 4:1–11)

Howbeit when he the Spirit of truth is come, he will guide you into all truth: for he shall not speak of himself: but whatsoever he shall hear, that shall he speak: and he will shew you things to come. (John 16:13–15)

The Holy Spirit receives from the Father and brings that word to you. He is there to teach you all things, to guide you, and to lead you.

But the Comforter, which is the Holy Ghost, whom the Father will send in my name, he shall teach you all things. (John 14:26)

The Shield of Faith

The shield of faith guards us against discouragement. It stops the fiery darts that the devil throws against us as he attacks with feelings of doubt, unbelief, hopelessness, and despair. The shield of faith is a powerful tool in our arsenal from God that stops every arrow, with faith and encouragement and hope that comes from God Almighty. It reminds us to call those things which are not as though they are!

The shield of faith can also remind us that we are the head and not the tail. We are seated in heavenly places with our Lord Jesus Christ, and the enemy is under our feet. This is the way that Jesus sees us. The shield of faith builds us up to look at ourselves the way that Jesus sees us. He sees us as strong and powerful. He sees us as victors, and we are seated together with him in the fight of faith. Faith is always important when we pray. The shield of faith helps us to see and know that the answers to our prayers are coming, even if they take a while to come. Even if deliverance takes a while to achieve the victory, we know that God is all powerful and will win the battle.

And Jesus answering saith unto them, Have faith in God. For verily I say unto you, That whosoever shall say unto this mountain, Be thou removed, and be thou cast into the sea; and shall not doubt in his heart, but shall believe that those things which he saith shall come to pass; he shall have whatsoever he saith. Therefore I say unto you, What things soever ye desire, when ye pray, believe that ye receive them, and ye shall have them. (Mark 11:22–24)

As we are looking for answered prayers, the shield of faith will remind us that there is nothing impossible for God, and there is nothing too small or great that God is not concerned about for our lives when it comes to answering our prayers.

The Gospel of Peace

Shodding our feet with the gospel of peace prepares us to have the peace of God for wherever we walk on this earth. This part of God's holy armor helps us stay in peace no matter what situations swirl around us and try to instill fear, anger, or confusion into our lives. We can be prepared with the gospel of peace that rises up inside of us to bring us stability and a sense of calmness in the midst of the storms of life through the good news of the gospel of Christ!

For example, someone gets angry at you, yells at you, and tells you off. God will remind you that he loves the person, and he reminds you to counteract that rage with forgiveness and love in order to overcome the evil inside. This forgiveness and love that we display can break the chains of those who are angry; it disarms the demons working inside of them. While people are yelling you may feel peace and are not shaken. But in this case, you did not get entangled in that fight. You may not even know why, but that armor is there, protecting you in this area.

> For charity shall cover the multitude of sins. (1 Peter 4:8)

The Lord can bring you peace when someone comes against you. He will remind you of this scripture in Matthew.

> Blessed are ye, when men shall revile you, and persecute you, and shall say all manner of evil against you falsely for my sake. (Matthew 5:11)

Using the whole armor of God protects us because the ways of mankind are not always God's ways. However, God's ways will give us direction, protection, insight, and victory. We need the whole armor of God, especially when doing spiritual warfare or deliverance. Demons during deliverance can scream out and make nasty remarks through the person you are delivering. It is very easy to get angry when that person is saying all kinds of nasty remarks. God will remind us that we are not battling flesh and blood. In other words, it is not that person speaking, but the demons and the powers of darkness. The full armor of God is vital to us as Christians.

Prayer and Fasting

> And when they were come to the multitude, there came to him a certain man, kneeling down to him, and saying, Lord, have mercy on my son: for he is lunatic, and sore vexed: for offtimes he falleth into the fire, and oft into the water. And I brought him to thy disciples, and they could not cure him. Then Jesus answered and said, O faithless and perverse generation, how long shall I be with you? Bring him hither to me. And Jesus rebuked the devil; and he departed out of him: and the child was cured from that very hour. Then came the disciples to Jesus apart, and said, Why could not we cast him out? And Jesus said unto them, Because of your unbelief: for verily I say unto you, if you have faith as a grain of mustard seed, Ye shall say unto this mountain, Remove hence to yonder place; and it shall remove; and nothing shall be impossible unto you. Howbeit this kind goeth not out but by prayer and fasting.
> —Matthew 17:14–21

In this story of the lunatic, the disciples could not cast the spirit out of the boy. The disciples asked why they could not cast out the spirit. Jesus said to them that it was because of their unbelief. He also explained that this kind only went out through prayer and fasting. We know now that certain spirits are only cast out when we add prayer and fasting to the mix. Jesus said that they could not cast the spirit out because of unbelief and a lack of faith, but he always gives us the answer afterward, and that is fasting.

Fasting helps us to destroy unbelief, and it helps us with our faith. I believe that fasting is a very powerful weapon in our arsenal to use in deliverance, which amps up the power of our prayers. Fasting gets our flesh out of the way and allows us to become stronger in the Holy Spirit. When we fast and pray and speak to the Holy Spirit, we are speaking spirit to Spirit, and we have fine-tuned ourselves into hearing the Holy Spirit's voice, not the voice of our own fleshly emotions. The Holy Spirit is not flesh; he is spirit. To hear him in a clearer way, we must be in an attitude of fasting in preparation for deliverance.

Binding the Strongman

> Or else how can one enter into a strong man's house,
> and spoil his goods, except he first bind the strong man?
> and then he will spoil his house.
> —Matthew 12:29

Jesus said that first you must bind up the strongman. In the US military there are different ranks, and there are different ranks in the spiritual realm. Identifying and binding the strongman will make a deliverance go much more smoothly. The strongman in a person's life is the one calling the shots to the other spirits of darkness. I have found that in deliverance, once the strongman is bound, the other spirits become confused and lose their power to fight.

Jesus didn't say to do this second or third. He said to first bind up the strongman. Now, this strongman can be witchcraft, sorcery, spiritism, black magic, voodoo, or something else. Whatever the form of witchcraft that the person has been involved with is what you bind up in the name of Jesus. It also could be religion, lying, or murder. There should always be prayer and fasting to find out the name of the strongman. Talking to the person who will be delivered and finding out all of what he or she has been involved with is very important.

In one deliverance, I spoke with a person, and in counseling with her, she had been involved in so many different kinds of witchcraft that she came prepared with ten pages of information about what she had dabbled in. She had everything she'd ever done in her life concerning the occult written down on paper. She wanted to be set free so badly that she came totally prepared. She had gone all over the world and had gotten involved in many types of witchcraft, curses, and spells. This was very helpful for her deliverance because she had been involved in so many demonic things in her life. She was set free and is doing very well to this day. All glory to God.

Binding and Loosing

> Verily I say unto you, Whatsoever ye shall bind on earth
> shall be bound in heaven: and whatsoever ye shall loose
> on earth shall be loosed in heaven.
> —Matthew 18:18

This is a key that Jesus gives to us to use. He says that if you bind something up on this earth, it will be bound up in heaven. We have to bind up in the name of Jesus and by the blood of Jesus. In other words, Jesus is saying that all of heaven is backing us up! We are supposed to bind up the enemy, and God the Father will bind him too. God will back up your words!

Jesus says that whatsoever you loose on this earth shall be loosed in heaven. Whenever I bind up a spirit, this scripture tells me that I need to loose something too. For example, if I bind up a lying spirit, at the end of my deliverance, I loose the spirit of truth into that person's life. If I am binding up the spirit of hatred and anger, I loose the Holy Spirit's love and forgiveness. Now I have counteracted what the devil's assignment was, replacing it with the opposite attribute that comes from the Holy Spirit. I cast out the evil and then pray for the good attributes of God to be poured into that person's life to replace it, and to lead them. It is the same thing when I pray over a person's home. I bind and break any curses and spirits out of that person's home. Then I loose the good, wholesome attributes of God and the Holy Spirit into that home. I bless the home and every room in the home, and I loose the Holy Spirit's fruits into that home.

> But the fruit of the Spirit is love, joy, peace, longsuffering, gentleness, goodness, faith, meekness, temperance,: against such there is no law. (Galatians 5:22–23)

Here is the listing of the fruits of the Holy Spirit. We need them in order to live lives of peace and love.

Filling the Vessel

If the vessel is empty, swept, and garnished, the Bible says that the enemy can come back with seven spirits more wicked than the first.

> When the unclean spirit is gone out of a man, he walketh through dry places, seeking rest, and findeth none. Then he saith, I will return into my house from whence I came out; and when he is come, he findeth it empty, swept, and garnished. Then goeth he, and taketh with himself seven other spirits more wicked than himself,

and they enter in and dwell there: and the last state of
that man is worse than the first. Even so shall it be with
this wicked generation. (Matthew 12:43–45)

If the vessel is empty after deliverance, and nothing has been prayed out
to refill the area that has been vacated, the demons can come in and fill
that place again in the future. This scripture says that it will be seven
times worse than the first, with seven demons more wicked than the
first. This also tells me that the person who has been delivered needs to
follow up. This person needs to read the word and fill himself or herself
with the Word of God for the deliverance to be successful. It is vitally
important to know that the person wanting deliverance is very serious
about what he or she is going to do, sincerely desiring to make that step
to follow Jesus Christ and make him the Lord of his or her life.

Those saved need to know that after being set free from the demonic,
in order for them to fill themselves with the Word of God to keep their
deliverance, and for the newly freed to stay strong, they will need to
read the Word of God and spend time with God daily after deliverance.
We do not want them to be empty and cleaned out, but never filled up
with the attributes of God to help them to overcome the temptations
that could follow.

Power of Agreement

As we see in scripture, Jesus sent the disciples out two by two.

> Again I say unto you, That if two of you shall agree on
> earth as touching anything that they shall ask, it shall
> be done for them of my Father which is in heaven. For
> where two or three are gathered together in my name,
> there am I in the midst of them. (Matthew 18:19–20)

> Where no council is, the people fall: but in the multitude
> of counsellors there is safety. (Proverbs 11:14)

I call this God's law of agreement. We are not islands unto ourselves. We need each other. God promises he will be with us, and his power will be there for us as we gather together. I always make sure that during deliverance, I have a team with me. Scripture tells us that in a multitude of counselors, there is safety.

I feel that it is very important to have people anointed and gifted in deliverance. I seek a team that works together, people who are full of faith, people who hear the voice of God, and people who are saturated with his power of truth. This is vitally important for successful deliverances. In the book of Acts, it was when the Church prayed, with all believing in unity, that powerful things happened.

> And they continued steadfastly in the apostles' doctrine
> and fellowship, and in breaking of bread, and in prayers.
> And fear came upon every soul: and many wonders and
> signs were done by the apostles. And all that believed
> were together, and had all things in common; And sold
> their possessions and goods, and parted them to all
> men, as every man had need. And they, continued daily
> with one accord in the temple, and breaking of bread
> from house to house, did eat their meat with gladness
> and singleness of heart, Praising God, and having
> favour with all the people. And the Lord added to the
> church daily such as should be saved. (Acts 2:42–47)

The unity and agreement between the people brought the miraculous from God, and it was very important just as it is today. We cannot allow the devil to divide us when doing deliverance or receiving deliverance, because it says in scripture that a house divided will not stand.

Do Not Believe Spirits

> Beloved, believe not every spirit, but try the spirits
> whether they are of God: because many false prophets
> have gone out into the world. Hereby know ye the Spirit
> of God: Every spirit that confesseth that Jesus Christ
> is come in the flesh is of God: And every spirit that
> confesseth not that Jesus Christ is come in the flesh is
> not of God: and this is that spirit of antichrist, whereof
> ye have heard that it should come; and even now already
> is it in the world.
> —1 John 4:1–3

John warned us to not believe spirits are going to be truthful. We should not believe the spirits of darkness. I have had people tell me to ask the spirit its name, and my conviction on this is that the spirit most likely will not tell the truth because it does not want to lose his home, and demons are liars.

> Ye are of your father the devil, and the lusts of your
> father ye will do. He was a murderer from the beginning,
> and abode not in the truth, because there is no truth in
> him. When he speaks a lie he speaks of his own: for he
> is a liar, and the father of it. (John 8:44)

We are clearly told that the devil is a liar and the father of it, so I do not put my trust in anything a demon may say through a person during deliverance.

Demons do not tell the truth. They are liars and deceivers. I do not ask their names or believe them because I have known them to lie. By understanding the tactics of my enemy, I know I must seek the Father for wisdom. In deliverance, I have learned to keep my eyes on God, not on the manifestations that I see or the words the spirits of darkness will speak. Demons may groan, call names, and even get physical in an attempt to bring fear. For example, with voodoo the whole aim of the enemy is to bring his prey into total fear and terror! He will kill that person through the fear and torment he brings faster than the curse.

Do Not Fear

The devil roams about like a roaring lion seeking prey to devour. He is not a lion, but he roars like a lion to instill fear.

God has not given us a spirit of fear but one of power love and a sound mind. The key is to not allow fear to enter into any deliverance, and to assure the person being delivered to not allow fear to take hold no matter what he or she experiences. Teach the person who will be delivered to totally trust in God and know that God is the all-powerful one. He is well above the power of Satan, and this reassurance is vitally important for the success of that deliverance. We need to teach that the devil has already been defeated through Jesus Christ and through the cross upon which Jesus died.

Assure the person who will be delivered that God is the final authority. He is fully in control. God, Jesus, and the Holy Spirit are all powerful to deliver because it is God delivering that person through you. We cannot take the credit for deliverance. Jesus lives in us and is doing the works through us through his name, which has all power over the enemy. The Word of God says that every knee shall bow and every tongue shall confess that he is Lord!

Perseverance in Prayer

Another tactic is that when we are praying against the demons of darkness, and we get the victory, a lie of the enemy is that it is all over and we won, so we don't have to pray anymore. But I will say it is never over. The devil doesn't take a vacation. Yes, you defeated the demons, but others can be sent to take their places, or they can wait for a more opportune time to attack again. It is always better to play offence rather than defense after the enemy has attacked.

When Jesus was tempted by the devil and defeated him, it explains in Luke 4:13 that the devil departed from him for a season, which means that he can come back at a later time. In another translation, the New Revised Standard Version, it says, "When the devil had finished every test, he departed from him until an opportune time." The devil looks for an opportune time to deceive you. Most likely it is when you are not paying attention!

> Fear not Daniel: for from the first day thou didst set thine heart to understand, and to chasten thyself before thy God, thy words were heard, and I am come for thy words. But the prince of the kingdom of Persia withstood me, one and twenty days: but lo, Michael, one of the chief princes, came to help me; and I remained there with the kings of Persia. (Daniel 10:12–13)

The angel is explaining that God heard his prayer from the very beginning, but there was a great battle in the heavens, and one of the principalities withstood him. This would be a demon that is over a whole territory. This was a strong spirit that was holding the angel back from bringing the message of God to Daniel to answer his prayers.

As Daniel continues to fast, Michael the archangel comes to assist in the fight. This angel brings to Daniel the vision and the answer to his prayer, telling him that this vision is for later times. At the end of giving Daniel this prophetic message for the end of days, the angel tells Daniel,

> Knoweth thou therefore I come unto thee? and now will I return to fight the prince of Persia: and when

I am gone forth, lo, the prince of Grecia shall come.
(Daniel 10:20)

This shows us that in battle, there are reinforcements that will come. There is warfare in the heavens, and angels are fighting on our behalf. This angel is withstood by the demon until an archangel named Michael assists him in defeating the demon spirit! Most people think the fight is over right there: the angel came and brought Daniel the message, and Daniel has the victory. But the angel gets through the battlefield and brings the message to Daniel because Daniel stayed persistent in his prayer.

Now, it is clearly shown that the battle is not over, because the angel himself declares that when he returns to heaven, the enemy has brought reinforcements of another major spirit high up in the chain of command to fight him. This is why the scriptures tell us, "We are to pray without ceasing!" (1 Thessalonians 5:17).

We also need to pray for discernment over our regions. We need discernment of what spirits and strongholds are over our states, cities, and towns. In our country, we are seeing more and more violence on a daily basis. It is not uncommon to hear of murders daily. It is not uncommon to hear of deadly riots and protests. There is a seemingly stronger division than ever before. It is going to take a praying Church to make a real change. The Church cannot fall into a spiritual sleep if we are going to win this war.

God has a lot to say about prayer. We are told to pray without ceasing. This means to pray all the time. We can pray when we are getting ready to go out in the morning, when we are cleaning our houses, and when we are taking a shower. While working at your job, you can pray. You can pray at any time and in almost any place, being an intercessor for God to do his will for his kingdom.

> The effectual fervent prayer of a righteous man availeth much. (James 5:16)

> My house shall be called a house of prayer. (Matthew 21:13)

Although the Church is a place of learning and healing, God calls his house the house of prayer. He places a high emphasis on prayer. Prayer changes everything! Prayer is finding the will of God. Prayer is finding out real answers from God. Prayer is receiving guidance and direction from God. And finally, prayer is receiving discernment if we ask God for it. This is an essential key for successful deliverance and spiritual warfare.

Gifts of the Holy Spirit

> For to one is given by the Spirit the word of wisdom; to another the word of knowledge by the same Spirit; To another faith by the same spirit; to another the gifts of healing by the same Spirit; To another the working of miracles; to another prophecy; to another discerning of spirits; to another divers kinds of tongues; to another the interpretation of tongues; But all these worketh that one and the selfsame Spirit, dividing to every man severally as he will.
> —1 Corinthians 12:8–11

Praying for the gifts of the Holy Spirit is very important. Pray for God to give you the word of wisdom, the word of knowledge, faith, healing, the working of miracles, prophecy, discernment of spirits, divers kinds of tongues, and interpretations of tongues. All of these gifts can be very helpful when doing deliverance and when operating in intercession.

A few years after I was saved, I realized that I needed to pray for discernment of spirits so that I could recognize what I was fighting. I also knew that if I was going to do deliverance or healing, I needed to know what I was casting out, and I also needed to have faith to cast it out. I needed to know what the person needed to be healed from and in what direction to go in order to help them. These gifts of the Holy Spirit are essential to being effective! I also needed to have discernment of the heart. This was revealed to me after I started praying for the gifts of the Holy Ghost. He said that I needed to know what needed to be healed. Every single day, I prayed for God to fill me with these gifts, and he was faithful to fill me with those gifts.

I know that discernment of the heart is not listed here. But if you look deeper into this scripture passage, in verses 4–6 you will notice that there are diversities of gifts, differences in administrations, and diversities of operations. These are all different because we are all unique, and our callings are unique and are specifically designed for us. I have always been a person who wants as much as I can get from God. He is the one who gives the gifting, and he makes the final decision, but I believe that he gives the gifts according to your hunger and how much you are willing to press into him to receive these gifts, and what you will need to have to fulfill the task that he has for your life. There is no limit to what you can ask for when it comes to wisdom and knowledge from him, as well as the gifs that you need to accomplish God's calling on your life!

The Incision of the Heart

God wants to make an incision into the hearts of his people. This will take a humble and contrite heart. The Word of God says, "A humble and contrite heart I will not despise." A cut hurts. I broke my Achilles tendon in 2010. It was broken in three spots and totally severed at my heel. My ankle was a mess. The doctor told me I had two choices. Either let it heal on its own—and it might never be totally normal—or have surgery on my ankle that would be painful but would have a more normal healing process; afterward, my ankle would be much stronger. I chose the surgery, which initially would be more painful and take a little longer to heal, but in the end would make my ankle much stronger. I am glad I elected to have the surgery because after the surgery, the doctor said my tendon was smashed in pieces. The doctor told me that he had put my ankle back together like it was a jigsaw puzzle. He told me that it would never have healed on its own.

The surgery that God wants to do in our hearts, and in the hearts of others, is painful too. To be healed of our hurts, we need to allow Jesus to bring us back to the point of our pain so that it can be confessed and released to the Lord. Our lives can be like a jigsaw puzzle. One hurt on top of the other can add up to fragmented pieces that cause our lives to feel totally confused and a mess. Only then can we be healed from our past hurts.

In the healing process, you may have to forgive someone who has injured you deeply. You may have to ask for forgiveness for offenses, resentment, and bitterness. Some hindrances to true healing and deliverance can include anger, rage, wrath, pride, haughtiness, revenge, spitefulness, envy, jealousy, manipulation, stubbornness, and control. All of these things are in opposition to the working of the Holy Spirit in a person's life. Repentance of these negative emotions are essential to healing.

A spirit of stubbornness in people can make them refuse to let go of their hurts. It will refuse to allow Jesus to come in. Sometimes people can be so comfortable about carrying their pain for so long that these hurts become a crutch. I have ministered to people who have told me that they have never had peace in their lives. I have heard some who say that peace to them is boring, and it scared them. Some have lived in confusion and torment, and they have not known anything else.

I know that people like this need healing at a slower pace that they can handle. They need a lot of explanation and patience about how God is going to change their lives. If they have never had peace and have never seen peace around them, they would not know that it is natural and good. All of this has to be explained. For some, we have to stand by their sides more than others. Some people I have ministered to have lived with such chaos, abuse, designed in their lives. This needs to be replaced with the Word of God, but for some, this may not happen overnight. For some whom we have ministered to, they have been mentally or physically abused; for some it was a short period in their lives, and for some it has been their whole lives. Eventually, step by step the Lord will change them from the inside out.

Individuals are unique in what they can handle and how fast that they can receive God's wonderful healing and deliverance. I have seen people with such deep hurts and wounds be healed. Broken lives were restored when they were ready to end their lives. Their spirits were restored to the way God originally intended their lives to be. Is it easy? No. It takes a lot of sacrifice from those who will help these people, and it took a lot of sacrifice from those who are receiving the counsel. It took a lot of time and a lot of effort. But it is so worthwhile when you are able to see a life that was in ruin be totally restored. The people can now see promise for their lives and a hopeful future!

Some healings take a lot of time. I have come across some people who have no one by their sides. The Church is all they have left. Some I have encountered have been hurt, mentally abused, and physically abused. They have been rejected or abandoned by people they trusted, going all the way back to their childhood. I have heard many say that the Church was their last hope and that if God could not help them, they were going to give up on life and kill themselves. Thankfully, God is the answer, and he is the healer and deliverer. He can change a heart in one second! He can deliver a person from a life time of wounds! He is the glory and the lifter of our heads! He can take the heaviness, depression, hopelessness, and despair out of you in a second, if you are willing to give it to him!

Some healings are immediate. Some healings may take much more time to totally be made whole again. It's not because God is not willing. He is very willing. But he will not give us more than we can bear. It all depends on the individuals and what they are willing to give up and open up about before the Lord, fully surrendering to God. I have seen deliverances where one word turned the whole thing around and brought tears, and God broke through their hearts by a simple phrase such as "God loves you!" The most important thing is that it is a revelation from God to be given to the person to whom you are ministering. People could have heard that word a thousand times, and it meant nothing, but when God gives it just at the right time with the power of the Holy Spirit, it now becomes personal, like a special message right from God to that person. My husband will often receive a loving word, or a word that only the person could know, and he will say it in a whisper. All of a sudden, the ice is broken off of the person's heart, and healing begins.

God has given us messages for people we are delivering that only he could know, and it can be a word that will save their lives. Many will be shocked and say, "How did you know?" At that point, they cannot deny God is in the room and personally dealing with them. It is important that we search God to guide us in deliverance and healing. I usually pray to God to give me a discernment of the heart for those I am going to minister to, and he is truly faithful to give that discernment. It is a prayer that you can do if you are called to deliverance ministry.

We have met many who are involved in sadomasochism. Some burn themselves, and some cut themselves. Some live in total darkness. When I saw that this was something that was becoming more common, I decided to go to the Internet and look up the terms *masochism* and *sadomasochism*.

> Sadomasochism is the giving or receiving of pleasure from acts involving the receipt or infliction of pain or humiliation. Practitioners of Sadomasochism may seek sexual gratification from their acts. While the terms sadist and masochist refer respectively to one who enjoys giving or receiving pain, practitioners of sadomasochism may switch between activity ad passivity. (Wikipedia)

Then I looked up masochism to see everything written about this disorder, and this is what I found.

> The masochist has been taught from an early age to hate himself/herself and consider themselves unworthy of love and worthless as a person. Consequently, he/she is prone to self-destructive, punishing, and self-defeating behaviors. Though capable of pleasure and possessed of social skills, the masochist avoids or undermines pleasurable experiences. He/she does not admit to

enjoying themselves, and seeks suffering, pain and hurt in relationships and situations, rejects help, and resents those who offer it. He/she actively renders futile attempts to assist or mitigate solve his/her problems and predicaments. These self penalizing behaviors are self purging: they intend to relieve the masochist of overwhelming, pent up anxiety. The masochist's conduct is equally aimed at avoiding intimacy and its benefit: companionship and support.

Masochists tend to choose people and circumstances that inevitably and predictably lead to failure, disillusionment, disappointment, and mistreatment. Conversely, they tend to avoid relationships, interactions, and circumstances that are likely to result in success or gratification. They reject, disdain, or even suspect people who consistently treat them well. Masochists find caring loving persons sexually unattractive. The masochist typically adopts unrealistic goals and this guarantees underachievement.

By researching deeply, I realized that for people involved in this lifestyle, their deliverance and counseling could be much more involved—but it's not impossible, because to God nothing is impossible. Not only is there the demonic end to this problem, but there are also deep-seeded problems birthed out of a whole life of teaching that had to be changed, many habitual acts that these people have grown accustomed to, and a whole life of wounds that need to be healed by the Lord. They also tend to sabotage themselves, and this can complicate things.

I noticed that many of those people could have a hatred for many things. Here is a list of things told to me by those who are into sadomasochism: an extreme hate for colors, hatred for men, hatred for women, hatred for animals, hatred of people, hatred of expressing love, hatred of those displaying joy, and hatred for flowers.

I believe that in preparing for deliverance, it is very important to find out if the people can remember one traumatic thing that stands out in their life that afterward brought this change into the demonic and into these destructive disorders. If they are receiving help from a doctor for the anxiety, I tell them to not stop this help they are receiving in that area.

I usually ask the person when things started to really get demonic in their lives, and usually there is something very traumatic that they couldn't deal with that brought them into the dark side. For some, they join a group that is involved in this, and the satanic aspect is a huge part of it. This is part of the game they played. Some were made to drink blood, and from there these people's lives could begin to spiral out of control. Some may only have one partner, but many could have several sexual partners. In some cases, they can be involved with a whole group at the same time.

For different sexual partners, this brings in many soul ties to all the individuals they have been involved with sexually.

> And said, For this cause shall a man leave father and mother, and shall cleave to his wife: and they twain shall be one flesh? Wherefore they are no more twain, but one flesh. What therefore God hath joined together let not man put asunder. (Matthew 19:5–6)

The joining of husband and wife, joins together their spirits and their souls as one in a holy union instituted by God. God has ordained this for only the married couple. This is why when people have been married for a very long time, they can finish each other's statements. They feel when the other partner is hurting. They are spiritually knitted and united together. When people outside of marriage have multiple partners, they are knitted together with them in the same way. The one thing that differs is that it is not a holy union, and it is not blessed by God. They are knitted together in their spirit and soul. These soul ties have to be broken in order to be set free from each individual partner with whom the person has been involved. They must repent of their involvement in fornication (meaning sex before marriage), and then they need to renounce all soul ties. I see people that receive immediate relief and freedom from that alone.

Forgiveness is the next step. If there are abusive relationships the people have been involved in, it is essential for them to be taught about how important it is to forgive, and to ask God's forgiveness for any unforgiveness they still have against those who have hurt them. Prayer for healing is needed for their broken spirits and for their wounded hearts.

> Then came Peter to him, and said, Lord, how oft shall my brother sin against me, and I forgive him? Till seven times? Jesus said unto him, I say not unto thee, Until seven times: but, Until seventy times seven. Therefore is the kingdom of heaven likened unto a certain king, which would take account of his servants. And when he had begun to reckon, one was brought unto him, which owed him ten thousand talents. But forasmuch as he had not to pay, his lord commanded him to be sold, and his wife, and children, and all that he had, and payment to be made. The servant therefore fell down, and worshipped him, saying, Lord, have patience with me, and I will pay thee all. Then the lord of that servant was moved with compassion, and loosed him, and forgave him the debt. But the same servant went out, and found one of his fellow servants, which owed

him an hundred pence: and he laid hands on him, and took him by the throat, saying, Pay me that thou owest. And his fellowservant fell down at his feet, and besought him, saying, Have patience with me, and I will pay thee all. And he would not: but went and cast him into prison, till he should pay the debt. So when his fellowservants saw what was done, they were very sorry, and came and told unto their lord all that was done. Then his lord, after that he had called him, said unto him, O thou wicked servant, I forgave thee all that debt, because thou desiredst me: Shouldest not thou also have had compassion on thy fellow servant, even as I had pity on thee? And his lord was wroth, and delivered him to the tormentors, till he should pay all that was due unto him. So likewise shall my heavenly Father do also unto you, if ye from your hearts forgive not every one his brother their trespasses. (Matthew 18:21–35)

Whose soever sins ye remit, they are remitted unto them: and whose soever sins ye retain, they are retained. (John 20:23)

For chains to be broken, forgiveness must take place! Chains are broken for you and for the person against whom you are holding unforgiveness. Unforgiveness holds us in bondage, in chains. Repentance for holding unforgiveness, offences, and bitterness is equally important!

Unforgiveness is a root, and the root has to be destroyed because it opens a door for other evil activity. Picture a tree that receives all of its nourishment from its roots. If the roots are diseased, the tree will be sick and diseased too, and eventually it will die. Or the roots can be healthy, supplied with fertilizer that feeds the tree and makes it healthy. If the roots are healthy and strong, the tree will flourish and grow with strong branches and healthy leaves and fruits. It is the same with each

40

of us. Our roots must be good, or else the rest of our very being will not be spiritually healthy.

In the story of Matthew 18, at the end of the story, the Lord says, "I forgave you all of your debt and was very angry and handed the wicked servant over to the tormentors!" Unforgiveness hands us over to many other spirits of darkness. It is a door to the demonic, and this door has to be closed in our lives if we are going to walk in freedom.

Once the unforgiveness is renounced and repented of, we are able to cast out all the other spirits that come into these people's lives because of that sin. Renouncing means to give up claim to, and to disown. Unforgiveness is the door that allows in everything else. There can be layers and layers of hurt, sin, and demons in a person's life that have to be disowned or renounced.

If a deep-seeded sin has been there for a very long time, it can fester into strong hostility, rage, violence, and revenge. All of these feelings can give way to more demons coming into the host. I have had people tell me that their hatred of others protects them from getting too close and getting hurt again. The demons in their minds say they are protecting them. Demons of hostility, anger, rage, and revenge are the guard dogs around them that keep the demonic going in their lives. They are there also to protect the much bigger demons from being cast out of the host.

Some people can have walls a mile high, and given the circumstances of the trauma they may have been through, it is understandable. But God doesn't say that we can pick and choose whom we will forgive. He simply says we should forgive, just as he has forgiven us and poured out his love upon those who receive him. That does not mean that you have to be a doormat for abuse. But it does mean that between you and God, you forgive that person from your heart. If you have difficulty in forgiving someone, ask God to help you forgive. Some pain is so deep that the person has to pray to be able to forgive through God's heart and with God's love. This is the prayer that I share with them to help them to be able to forgive. It is not just a suggestion from the Lord; it is a command. Unforgiveness will destroy us well before it will ever destroy our enemies! They will go on their way, having fun and not knowing or caring that someone else has feelings of unforgiveness towards them. The one it really hurts is you!

I would like to say that I know such subjects can be very uncomfortable, but we must realize that it is happening in our society. I have seen it, and it is becoming more common. It is something that we cannot ignore. More people are getting involved in Satanism nowadays, and it is something that not too many people want to talk about. But for those who find themselves in such deep darkness and want to come out of it, there has to be people who are willing (just as Jesus Christ was) to set the captives free! Some of the spirits that could be involved in someone entangled in sadomasochism are control, manipulation, Jezebel, anger, hostility, resentment, hatred, violence, spirits of Satanism, and blood drinking of sacrifices, These have to be repented of and renounced. If people made a pact with the devil, this also has to be renounced. The strongman of Satanism has to be renounced and cast out, and this should be done first.

> Or else how can one enter into a strong man's house,
> and spoil his goods, except he first bind the strong man?
> and then he will spoil his house. (Matthew 12:29)

If they have made a pact with the devil, and it is renounced and broken, the shackles the devil had on them are broken and removed. Shackles of heaviness, confusion, hatred, and even rage can be lifted off of people.

Finally, the people we have dealt with concerning sadomasochism were also repented of, renounced, and casted out in the name of Jesus Christ. Everything we do in deliverance, we do in the name of Jesus Christ.

There is power in that name! The demons have to bow to that name, and so we do not have to fear. God is in control during deliverance. He wants that person set free more than we do. He loves them deeply, and as we cast these spirits out of a person, we can rest assured that God is backing us up, helping us to have an effective deliverance and to ultimately set that person free. We have seen people set free: the torment and rage are gone, and they have the peace and love of God taking over their lives.

It is always important to pray that after they are delivered, God should fill them with his Holy Spirit. I also pray for God to fill them with his love, joy, peace, and happiness, as well as his strength and guidance, so they can stay strong with God. Now, all of this does not happen in one day. This all may happen over a period of time. Our patience and encouragement through this time is vitally important.

The Spoken Curse

Thou shalt also decree a thing, and it shall be established unto thee: and the light shall shine upon thy ways.
—Job 22:28

The Bible teaches us that there is power in our words. If we decree a thing, it shall be established unto us. Whether it is good or bad, what we decree will change our lives. God's Word says so. Think of your words as containers of power.

Behold, we put bits in the horses' mouths, that they may obey us; and we turn about their whole body. Behold also the ships, which though they be so great, and are driven of fierce winds, yet are they turned about with a very small helm, whithersoever the governor listeth. Even so the tongue is a little member, and boasteth great things. Behold, how great a matter a little fire kindleth! And the tongue is a fire, a world of iniquity: so is the tongue among our members, that it defileth the whole body, and setteth on fire the course of nature; and it is set on fire of hell. For every kind of beasts, and of birds, and of serpents, and of things in the sea, is tamed, and hath been tamed of mankind: But the tongue can no man tame; it is an unruly evil, full of deadly poison. Therewith bless we God, even the Father; and therewith

curse we men, which are made after the similitude of
God. Out of the same mouth proceedeth blessing and
cursing. My brethren, these things ought not so to be.
(James 3:3–10)

In this passage, our tongues are compared to the helm of a ship. The
helm is very small, but as it turns, it can turn around a huge ship. It's
also like the bit in a horse's mouth turns the whole body of a horse. Our
tongues are the same way. Our tongues can defile our whole bodies,
according to James. What could defile our bodies? Negative words
against the plans and the will of God for our lives, negative words
against our own health, negative words against our own finances, and
negative words against our own success or relationships and friendships.
Through our lives, we are shaped by either positive, encouraging words
or negative, hurtful, and destructive words. Yes, words do have an effect
on our lives.

James states that our tongues set on fire the course of nature, and it is
set on fire of hell. So why would our tongues be set on fire by hell? Well,
it certainly would not be set on fire if it had no effect on us.

The end of this scripture tells us that we bless God the Father but curse
the men who are made after God's likeness. Then it explains that we
can have blessing coming out of our mouths, or cursing. It does matter
what we say over our own lives, and it does matter what people have
decreed over us throughout our lives from the day that we were born.

Some parents tell their children that they will never amount to anything,
or they can never come out of poverty, or they are poor and will die
poor. Declaring that you will be sick over and over, or that you have no
money to do anything, are declarations over your life, and James says
that these words or curses are steering the course of nature around us,
swaying situations, people, and relationships around you. This does
not mean that if a person has a cold, you deny that he or she is sick. It

simply means that you deny its right to stay there, and you believe in the Lord to heal.

When I broke my Achilles tendon, the doctors said I would never walk again. I knew it was broken and shattered, and I went to therapy and had two surgeries on it. The whole time, I continued to believe and confess that I was being healed and would walk again. Speaking positive words, declaring, and decreeing positive, encouraging, victorious proclamations over our lives can steer our future into success and victory. God's promises are positive, such as all things are working together for the good for those who love God and are called according to his purposes. We are then aligning our faith toward the scriptural promises of God's Word for our lives. Our self-esteem is created through positive or negative comments made in our lives.

> And the whole earth was of one language, and of one speech. And it came to pass as they journeyed from the east, that they found a plain in the land of Shinar; and they dwelt there. And they said one to another, Go to, let us make brick and burn them throughly. And they had brick for stone, and slime had they for mortar. And they said go to, let us build a city and a tower, whose top may reach unto heaven; and let us make us a name, lest we be scattered abroad upon the face of the whole earth. And the LORD came down to see the city and the tower, which the children of man builded. And the LORD said, Behold, the people is one, and they have all one language; and this they began to do: and now nothing will be restrained from them, which they have imagined to do. Go to, let us go down, and there confound their language, that they may not understand one another's speech. So the LORD scattered them abroad from thence upon the face of all the earth: and

they left off to build the city. Therefore is the name of it called Babel; because the LORD did there confound the language of all the earth: and from thence did the LORD scatter them abroad upon the face of all the earth. (Genesis 11:1–9)

The Lord says in this story that because the people were speaking all the same thing and had the same language, there was nothing impossible unto them. They were strong and powerful, even though it was something that was not pleasing to God or in his will. God's answer to the problem was to scatter the people and confound their language, making it so that they could not all agree and decree and proclaim the same thing. The Lord confused their speech to defeat their plan of erecting a building up to heaven. At that time, it says that the whole world had the same language. That means that there were nonbelievers involved who could speak and have the power to achieve something by being in unity and by speaking forth their plans.

Many people who have come to me for deliverance have been knocked down by someone whom they looked up to and depended on, and those words cut like a knife into their hearts. Through one situation after another in their lives, they were knocked down and almost destroyed. The words of parents, teachers, friends, co-workers, and bosses made an extreme impact on these individuals. Their hearts were wounded, their spirits broken, and their self-esteem was knocked down to nothing. Other people's words convinced them that they were whatever they were told they were! But as they confess these hurts to the Lord, and renounced these words that were declared over them, and asked for Jesus Christ to heal them, we broke those words of negativity and broke their effects, and we saw healing and deliverance. A broken person can be totally healed through the finished work of the cross.

At that point, they were encouraged to speak encouraging scriptures over their lives that counteracted those negative words spoken over them, building up their faith in God. Then I had them repent for all the negative words that they had spoken over their own lives, renouncing them.

For example, if they constantly said that they could never be successful, I would give them a scripture like this.

> I can do all things through Christ which strengtheneth
> me. (Philippians 4:13)

God's Word is so uplifting, encouraging, and full of healing if we confess his Word as faithfully as we did the negativity we once proclaimed. God is the creator, and in Genesis he created the whole world by speaking. He spoke, and it was created. Yes, he is God, but he said that we were made after his likeness, and he now dwells in us. We have the capacity to declare the will of God and have a bright future through God, by our words. This is called blessing instead of cursing.

> For I know the thoughts that I think toward you, saith
> the LORD, thoughts of peace, and not of evil, to give
> you an expected end. (Jeremiah 29:11)

This is just one example of what God thinks about us. He has thoughts of peace and not of evil, and he seeks to give us a future that he has already planned. He wants to give us an expected end and a bright, new, successful future. This does not mean we will never have problems in life, but God will see us through those problems. Our job is to believe him and not doubt that what he promises, he is able to perform in our lives. We simply need to stand on the promises of his scriptures, confess, and believe what God has to say about our lives. We are precious to him. He loves us, cares about us, and wants the very best for each and every one of us. He wants us to not only be healed but also be made whole!

I have heard people declare they are fearful of so many things. I have heard them say over and over again that they are fearful of heights, of speaking in front of crowds, of water, or of death.

> For God hath not given us the spirit of fear; but of power,
> and of love, and of a sound mind. (2 Timothy 1:7)

God's word says the opposite! He says he did not give us a spirit of fear, but of power, love, and a sound mind. What I have noticed from those who declare negative things over their lives is that the problem only gets worse. The more they confess this into their lives, the more they are aligning themselves with what Satan has to say about them, instead of what God has to say about their lives. They are believing in the worst instead of believing in God's best and God's blessings. I used to have a fear of crowds, but as I came to God, he quickly told me to stop it. He then told me to repent of it, renounce it, and start speaking out that I no longer had fear. I did not have fear of anything! Over a period of time, this changed. I no longer had any fear of crowds. That fear was defeated!

I have had many people come to me with fear, and after they renounced it and renounced what they had declared all their lives, it was broken. They healed and received deliverance in that area of their lives.

Jesus came to set the captives free. Think of these negative words—or as it says in James 3:3–10, a curse—as something that has chains attached, or shackles. They stop a person from advancing in life. But once these people are brought before the Lord, renounce and repent of and their hearts, and are healed through the blood of Jesus Christ, they are set free and the chains are finally broken.

This is a prayer that can be used to receive freedom and healing from negative words and curses.

Father God, I come to you, and I repent for ever speaking anything negative over my life. I ask for your forgiveness, and for you to cleanse me of everything that came into my life because of those words. I renounce negativity of every kind, and I choose to stand on the promises of God for my life. I also break and renounce every single negative word of defeat, lack, depression, fear, guilt, shame, and condemnation that anyone else ever spoke over my life. Parents, teachers, friends, co-workers, bosses, acquaintances, and anyone who ever spoke negatively against me—I break and renounce those words in the name of Jesus Christ. I ask for your healing for the wounds that were placed into my heart, and that you will break every chain and every shackle that was placed over my life by those negative words. I now break these words off of the course of nature for my life, and I release into my life the blessings of God over my future. I loose into my life joy, happiness, peace, patience, hope, and faith in Jesus's name. Amen.

Family Line Curses

For I the Lord thy God am a jealous God visiting the iniquity of the fathers upon the children unto the third and fourth generation of them that hate me; and showing mercy unto thousands that love me and keep my commandments.
—Exodus 20:5–6

A family line curse is something passed down from one generation to another because of the sins of the father through the family lineage! Sins of witchcraft, unbelief, false doctrine, adultery, and murder are just a few of the sins that can be passed down from generation to generation. If it is never repented of, then it continues to be passed down as a frustration that affects the children. Notice that Exodus 20:5–6 says the iniquity is passed down to the third and fourth generation. If it is passed down to the third and fourth generation and is not repented of and cleansed, it goes on to the next third and fourth generation, and so on.

Families who have had murders in their bloodlines that have not been repented of will notice that their children go through things in their lives. It can be calamity, premature death, abandonment, abuse, alcoholism, or drug addiction. This is only an example of one sin and the different things that can come into the family because of the curse. It could be a different sin, like alcoholism, and then you will notice that the children and the children's children will often have the same problem with alcoholism. They want to stop but have a harder time stopping because it is a curse handed down through the family. Not all difficulties in life are a family line curse, but certainly this could be a root that should be looked at through counseling. Many times simply repenting of the sins passed down in the heritage can bring extreme healing.

When I came to the Lord in my early twenties, I had a lot of trouble with my heart. I had been to heart doctors for most of my life and was told that by the time I was thirty I would have open-heart surgery. Just before getting saved, I remember going in ambulances on a weekly basis to the emergency room because of my heart.

After I accepted Jesus into my heart as my Lord and Savior, I was then asked about my family lineage. I had explained about some of the sins in my family. I was guided into repenting of those sins and breaking off those curses going all the way back to Adam and Eve. I remember it was like a stack of bricks was taken off of my chest! I received an immediate healing of my heart problems, and I have never had those problems ever again. It is now more than thirty-five years later, and I have never had heart surgery.

Later in my walk, the Lord revealed even more things that he wanted to set me free. Many times God will do things in steps and stages. I have heard people say that when they came to Jesus and asked him into their hearts, they repented of their sins, and that is all they should have to do. Although we ask for forgiveness and repent of our sins, when we first come to the Lord, we are still learning what sin is. Even later in our walks, we are still learning! We can say the words, not know what we are sorry about, and continue sinning.

As I came to the Lord and accepted Jesus into my heart, I repented of my sins and asked God to cleanse me of all of my sins. I remember feeling so much cleaner and lighter. I continued to practice some occult practices that I was used to doing, and I thought there was nothing wrong with it. I also remember continuing to pray to the Mother Mary and trusting in dead saints to deliver me in situations. I said the words, "I repent!" But I did not know what sin was and what I was repenting of, so I continued the same way as when I came to the Lord. Although I wanted so much to please God, I didn't know what pleased God. It wasn't until I continued to read, went to Bible studies, and learned about God to find out what God liked and didn't like that I fully understood what sin was. I know that through this process, some things changed in my life right away as soon as I got saved. There were other things that I got delivered from through a process of time, learning, and gaining understanding; I was set free more and more.

Even after deliverance, it is important to seek the Lord and ask him to continue teaching and showing you anything you need to know that will help you be set free.

> Again, the kingdom of heaven is like unto treasure hid
> in a field; the which when a man hath found, he hideth,
> and for joy thereof goeth and selleth all that he hath,
> and buyeth that field. (Matthew 13:44)

Receiving all that God has for us in his kingdom is like a treasure that is hidden in a field. We are the ones who must search heart for all that he has for us. What is in heaven that we would want from God? God wants to give us peace, joy, happiness, love, healing, miracles, success, and deliverance! He wants to set free the captives. Above all things, people do not want torment in their lives, and a curse can bring torment, sickness, sadness, disease, and even death. God wants for us to have a long, healthy, happy lives with him at the center of it all. This does not mean that we will never encounter any problems of any kind, but it does mean that we will have God to be there with us and see us through whatever we face.

As we search the heart of the Father, we can learn and receive more and more of the answers to unlock the freedom he wants to give us for our lives.

> Ask, and it shall be given you; seek, and ye shall find; knock, and it shall be open unto you: For every one that asketh receiveth; and he that seeketh findeth; and to him that knocketh it shall be opened. (Matthew 7:7–8)

Searching for the truth is an onward effort that God tells us to do. We are to ask, seek, and knock on the door of his heart. We must search for the things of God that will bring us freedom like they are fine pearls! We should ask God to show us any sin passed down in our heritage that can be a curse following us, hindering us, and even harassing our lives! Write it down on paper. This can be important, especially in the beginning of a person being set free. As the Lord begins to show us, we write it down, and now we know what has been covered and what may still need to be done. God is a God of organization, not of confusion, and so writing down all the things that God shows to you can be extremely helpful in obtaining information.

Researching and asking questions about your family lineage is very helpful. Things to do with your nationality, religion, and the lives of your ancestors will give you much-needed information to help in setting you or someone else free. If you do not know those things and cannot obtain this information, then ask, seek, and find from the Lord for his insight into what you need to know. I will give an example.

Say that your heritage was involved in witchcraft as a part of its lineage. Not only will that curse of witchcraft will have to be broken off of you, but also family lineage curses will have to be repented of and then broken off of your life.

There are nationalities of many kinds that have witchcraft as a part of their heritage. Each nationality can have its own brand of witchcraft. Some nationalities do witchcraft over their babies right after they are born. They may not even know that it is witchcraft they are doing. But these things are important to know and to have broken off of our lives if we are to truly be set free.

The people you are delivering could have anger problems, and after deliverance, they may still have a problem with anger. They don't want to operate in anger, but it seems to pull at them, like it is hovering over them. They may fall to this anger problem over and over. You may want to look into the family lineage to see what has been inherited by the new believers. It could be that back in the family tree, there was marital abuse, division in the family, unforgiveness between family members, adultery, fornication, and so on. These are roots that need to be dug up, repented of, broken off, and even cleansed by the blood of Jesus Christ.

These are only a few examples to help you understand how to search for what problems could be in your life, or for the person on whom you are doing deliverance.

One man whom we did deliverance on was having a serious problem with lying. Although he repented of it, he said that no matter how much he tried, he would mean to say one thing but instead say something else, and he would uncontrollably lie about things. He was very upset about this sin. He cried about it and felt horrible that he was letting God down. As he shared what he was going through with me, he also said that his father had lied a lot, and he noted that lying was something that happened a lot in his family.

I explained to him that this could be a family line curse, and I told him to repent of his forefathers' sin concerning the lying. I had him renounce this sin and renounce the demons that came into his life through the sins of his forefathers. We casted the spirit of lying out of his life, and after that, he was set free and no longer had that problem.

Another person who came to us for deliverance was being tormented in her mind. It came out that her father had been with many women, and there was a lot of resentment, bitterness, and unforgiveness. The sins of her forefathers of fornication and of the adultery had to be repented of, the curses of it had to be broken, and the demons of adultery and fornication had to be cast out. Then this person was delivered of her tormentors. We prayed for God's peace and love to fill her and heal her heart from what her family member had done.

Here is a prayer for the deliverance of family line curses.

> Father, I come to you in the name of Jesus, and I repent of the sins of my forefathers and break the family line curses of _____ off of my life. I break the curse of _____ in the name of Jesus going all the way back to Adam and Eve, and I ask for your forgiveness for the sins of my forefathers. I ask you to forgive me of all of these sins and cleanse me from anything that came into my life because of these curses and sins, which were demonic. I renounce all demons that came into my life through these family line curses, and I cast those spirits out of my life in Jesus's name. Thank you, Father God, for delivering me and setting me free in Jesus's name. Amen.

Breaking Soul Ties

Marriage is honorable in all, and the bed undefiled: but
whoremongers and adulterers God will judge.
—Hebrews 13:4

Marriage is the institution created by God that is blessed. God created
the covenant of marriage to be holy. The marriage bed is to be holy,
with one man and one woman to become one under God.

For this cause shall a man leave his father and mother,
and shall be joined unto his wife, and they two shall
become one flesh. (Ephesians 5:31)

Here in Ephesians, the word of God says to us that as a man is joined
to his wife, they become one flesh. But many look at that scripture and
cannot understand how this could possibly be true. They may say, "Well,
I am still in my flesh, and my husband is in his flesh, so how can that
be true?" But here, the scripture is saying that the two shall become one
in union of the holy matrimony, which is a covenant before God where
their souls are united as one. This is why after they have been married
for years, they can finish each other's sentences. Spouses feel when the
other is hurting because they have been combined to each other in a
spiritual way through the power of God.

When they come to God, many have been sexually involved with
multiple partners. They have slept together outside of marriage, and

they have combined their souls in the same fashion. One person could have been with a partner, break up with that partner, go to another partner, and so on! Now that person has combined his soul with that partner, and the partner he has been involved with has been involved with other partners. Spiritually, confusion starts to enter. These people take on all the curses that are on that person and throughout their family lineage, and now they have their own demons and the other partner's demons. As these partners break up, this can be the reason why they cannot get prior partner out of their minds. They are still spiritually connected to prior partners, through a soul tie. Many times even if they were the ones who broke off the relationship, and even if they don't like the old partners anymore, they can be tormented with the thoughts of prior partners because their souls have been combined. They entered into the sexual bond that really is meant only for the holy marriage bed with one partner for life.

Sex outside of marriage is a sin. Sexual sin opens the doors to the demonic. Sex outside of marriage is called fornication.

> But fornication, and all uncleanness or covetousness,
> let it not be once named among you, as becometh saints.
> (Ephesians 5:3)

Fornication is sin, and it can be repented of! We can repent from our hearts unto God for involving ourselves in relationships outside of marriage. The person wanting to be delivered can renounce all soul ties and ask Jesus Christ to break them off of his of her life. I usually tell the person to repeat after me so that I am in agreement with the person who wants to be set free. I will then tell the person to name those whom he has been involved with when he gets into the privacy of his own home, between God and that person alone, because sometimes this can be a very embarrassing thing to mention to someone else. I also tell him to renounce any spirits that came into his life through being with that person (or people), as well as family lineage sins and spirits.

> Know ye not that your bodies are the members of Christ? Shall I then take the members of Christ and make them the members of an harlot? God forbid. What? know ye not that he which is joined to an harlot is one body? For two saith he, shall be one flesh. But he that is joined unto the Lord is one spirit! Flee fornication. Every sin that a man doeth is without the body; but he that committeth fornication sinneth against his own body. (1 Corinthians 6:15–18)

The passage makes it absolutely clear that not only do you become one with that person, but you become one with the sexually sinful nature. It says that he who is joined to the harlot is one with her body!

These soul ties are important to break in order to receive true freedom. I am not saying that you will see fireworks as you break them, but you will certainly notice a difference afterward.

One person whom I ministered to was having extreme problems, including emotional issues and demonic problems. I asked that person when she started to notice these issues in her life. The person named what age she was. I then asked what traumatic thing happened to her around that time. As the person thought, she realized that it was at the same time she had been raped. The rape was very traumatic and brought in huge fear. I explained all of this had to be brought to God and healed. All the emotional pain and condemnation that the devil was placing on this person was brought to the Lord, broken, and healed. Then I explained that this was a soul tie that had to broken. We took these soul ties to the Lord and broke them, and this person who had been tormented for her whole life was set free. Praise God!

Each deliverance is different, depending on what the person has been through. Each person is unique. But God is the one who directs us to the answers. He will guide us if we ask him to reveal what has to be done. He is faithful and wants to see his children set free.

Here is a prayer of deliverance to break soul ties.

> Father, I come to you in the name of Jesus. I repent of the sin of fornication, and I ask you to forgive me of this sin. I ask you to wash me with the precious blood of your son, Jesus Christ. Father, I break the soul ties between me and anyone I have been with sexually, outside of the Word of God. I renounce all spirits that came into my life because of my this sin, and I renounce all spirits that came into my life because of the sins that were on my partner or partners. I cast them out of my life. Lord, I ask you to help me to walk in a way that is pleasing to you. I thank you for setting me free in Jesus's name. Amen.

Idols, Statues and Graven Images

Thou shalt not make unto thee any graven image, or
any likeness of anything that is in heaven above, or that
is in the earth beneath, or that is in the water under the
earth: Thou shalt not bow down thyself to them, nor
serve them: for I the LORD thy God am a jealous God,
visiting the iniquity of the fathers upon the children
unto the third and fourth generation of them that hate
me; and showing mercy unto thousands of them that
love me, and keep my commandments.
—Exodus 20:4–6

In the *Vines Dictionary,* the Greek Hebrew translation of *graven* is
explained as "to engrave, mark, stamp. Image is translated as a shape,
form, or appearance."

Take ye therefore good heed unto yourselves; for ye saw
no manner of similitude on the day that the LORD
spake unto you in Horeb out of the midst of the fire:
Lest ye corrupt yourselves, and make you a graven
image, the similitude of any figure, the likeness of male
or female, The likeness of any beast that is on the earth,
the likeness of any winged fowl that flieth in the air,
The likeness of anything that creepeth on the ground,
the likeness of any fish that is in the waters beneath

the earth: And lest thou lift up thine eyes unto heaven, and when thou seest the sun, and the moon, and the stars, even all the host of heaven, shouldest be driven to worship them, and serve them, which the LORD thy God hath divided unto all nations under the whole heaven. (Deuteronomy 4:15–19)

Deuteronomy explains to us God's feelings about statues, idols, and graven images. He says to take heed to yourself and to not corrupt yourself by having these things or worshiping them.

Take heed unto yourselves, lest ye forget the covenant of the LORD your God, which he made with you, and make you a graven image, or the likeness of anything, which the LORD thy God hath forbidden thee. (Deuteronomy 4:23)

They that make a graven image are all of them vanity; and their delectable things shall not profit; and they are their own witnesses; they see not, nor know; that they may be ashamed. (Isaiah 44:9)

God gives very strong commands about graven images, idols, and statues, letting us know that he forbids it. He even goes so far as to let us know exactly what things we are not supposed to make.

For the person who may use the argument that he does not worship these items or bow down to them, the scripture also says not to make or create them. God holds us accountable for creating it and forming it.

Manasseh was twelve years old when he began to reign, and he reigned fifty and five years in Jerusalem: but did that which was evil in the sight of the LORD, like unto the abominations of the heathen, whom the LORD had cast out before the children of Israel. For he built again the high places which Hezekiah his father had broken down, and he reared up altars for Baalim, and made groves, and worshipped all the host of heaven, and served them. Also he built altars in the house of the LORD, whereof the LORD had said, In Jerusalem shall my name be forever. And he built altars for all the host of heaven in the two courts of the house of the LORD. And he caused his children to pass through the fire in the valley of the son of Hinnom: also he observed times, and used enchantments, and used witchcraft, and dealt with a familiar spirit, and with wizards: he wrought much evil in the sight of the LORD, to provoke him to anger. And he set a carved image, the idol which he had made, in the house of God, of which God had said to David and to Solomon his son, In this house, and in Jerusalem, which I have chosen before all the tribes of Israel, will I put my name for ever: Neither will I any more remove the foot of Israel from out of the land which I have appointed for your fathers; so that they will take heed to do all that I have commanded them, according to the whole law and the statutes and the ordinances by the hand of Moses. So Manasseh made Judah and the inhabitants of Jerusalem to err, and to do worse than the heathen, whom the LORD had destroyed before the children of Israel. (2 Chronicles 33:1–9)

It is said here with the life of Manasseh that he did evil in the sight of the Lord. Witchcraft is evil in God's sight; it causes people to do evil acts, which this scripture explains. It says that they did more evil than the people they had destroyed in battle! He did soothsaying, which is foretelling the future. He consulted with familiar spirits and mediums, which is calling up of the dead, speaking to the dead, and speaking to spirits to bring information. He did witchcraft, which is the use of spells, potions, and curses. He also consulted wizards.

It says at the end of this story that the Lord spoke to Manasseh and his people, but they would not listen, and so the Lord brought up against him captains of the army of Assyria, which took him with hooks, bound him with bronze fetters, and carried him off to Babylon. He was greatly afflicted, begged the Lord, humbled himself greatly before the God of his fathers, and prayed to him. It says that God received his prayer and repentance and brought him back to Jerusalem! In 2 Chronicles 33:15, it says that Manasseh took away the strange gods and the idol from out of the house of the Lord, as well as all the altars that he had built in the mount of the house of the Lord and in Jerusalem, and he cast them out of the city. It is important to note that not only did he take down the graven images, but he also took them out of the city! After casting the evil objects out, in 2 Chronicles 33:16 it says, "And he repaired the altar of the LORD, and he sacrificed peace offerings, and thank offerings, and commanded Judah to serve the LORD God of Israel!"

In this passage, it clearly explains how angry God was with doing witchcraft and sorcery, having graven images, and being involved with demonic practices. It also shows us that there were consequences for Manasseh as he practiced the occult.

Idols such as Ouija boards have a spirit attached to the board. When using this so-called game, you ask the spirit about your future. Eight balls are another game where you ask questions from the demonic spirits to tell your future. Dragon statues are representative of Satan. Buddha statues, which are another god, sometimes have a ritual attached or written on the bottom of the statue. There are some statues that have prayers to spirit guides, which open the door to the demonic. Statues of imps, dwarfs, gnomes, and gargoyles are not just some cute thing that you and I have seen in Disney movies. They are not harmless—they are something very demonic, are associated with Satanism, and leave a very dangerous opening for the devil to come through against the person desiring to be set free.

We had some friends ask us to help a girl who was being tormented and haunted. At night, demon imps and dwarves were running over her bed. She was petrified! One of the friends explained that this girl received Jesus as her Lord and Savior, and after receiving Jesus into her heart, everything got worse. She heard loud crashes at night. Things on her walls were crashing to the floor. This girl was afraid to go to sleep at night and was in total terror. They did have statues of the very things this young girl was seeing running over her bed, but something much deeper was going on with her.

We went to see her at the request of the mother, but when we arrived, the Lord revealed that one of the problems was stemming from the mother. That the mother was involved in what was going on. We talked to the mother and shared what God had revealed to us. That was when we learned that the mother had given her daughter over to her husband, who was into Satanism and had put this girl on the altar of Satan, dedicating her to Satan. These actions had to be repented of by the mother first, and the mom had to reclaim her daughter for the Lord. She had given permission and assistance in handing this girl over to Satan, and so the rituals and curses that were done over her had to be broken. The dedication and the pact with the devil, along with all curses, spells, and rituals, had to be broken in the name of Jesus—by the mom. She was the root of the whole thing, and as a new believer she had to reclaim her daughter for God.

The tormentors were bound up in the form of these imps and dwarves and cast out of the home. We were very careful to not cause the girl any more trauma. Most of what was done was done through the mom, and the rest was done in a very gentle manner for the girl's sake. Then the power of God's love and peace had to be loosed in the name of Jesus into the home and into this girl's life. As I tell this story, I am sure that it sounds as though this all took place in a short period of time, but before we even went there, we had prayed for weeks and fasted, seeking the Lord deeply in this matter. I remembered that our main objective before anything else would be to calm her and instill into her that she was going to be okay and that God was watching over her. Sensitivity and discernment were very important for us as we dealt with this. When speaking with the mom, we spoke away from the girl in a separate area. This was important so that we would not escalate her fears. All the statues of the imps and dwarves that they owned were representative of what she had gotten involved in, and they had to be removed and destroyed for this girl to be set free.

We told her mom, "To be set free, you need to remove the ungodly items. That is still your choice. We can only offer advice. We cannot force you to get rid of the objects, and God will not violate your will." We also explained that if they were not willing to get rid of the demonic objects, we would not be involved in any deliverance at all, for the reason of protecting them and us. If there are demonic objects which are idols or graven images, it gives the demons the right to be there. We needed to take away the demons rights to be there and close the open doors for the demonic; that this would make everything in this deliverance smoother and easier.

The sun, moon, and stars with the faces engraved in them are another New Age form. They have the eyes and the mouth engraved into the item to signify that the form is alive, to give credence to the object that it is a living god. New Age in itself is the worship of nature instead of God. The trees, sun, moon, and stars are their gods to trust and to worship.

> Idol. 1. An image of a god, used as an object of worship.
> 2. Any object of ardent or excessive devotion. (*Webster's New World Dictionary*)

An idol could be also called a good luck charm. You use the item to protect you instead of trusting in the Lord. These trinkets can range from four-leaf clovers to dead saint medals that you wear in the hope that they will protect you. Mother Mary medals are items people use by making them into a form that they can wear, hoping to bring them luck. Rosaries with crucifixes on them are used to do a ritual prayer to the Mother Mary instead of going right to God or to Jesus Christ through his blood, which he shed on the cross of Calvary for me and for you. Jesus's name is above every name, and the scriptures explain that he is the mediator that we can go through between man and God.

> For there is one God, and one mediator between God
> and men, the man Christ Jesus. (1 Timothy 2:5)

Jesus is not still on the cross. He was resurrected and is alive! He is no longer dead! The scriptures clearly state to not make unto you any graven image from anything that is from the heavens above. When we come to Christ, it is time to take him off the cross. Our victory is in the fact that he is no longer on the cross but has risen from the dead. If he had stayed on the cross, which was what the devil wanted and thought was going to happen, then that would have been the defeat of Jesus. But death couldn't hold him! Death could not defeat him! It is the resurrection power that gives us the victory. It is the empty cross that gives us the victory. Hallelujah!

Horoscope medallions are another engraved image that is not of God. The horoscopes are a look into the future, based on psychics who foretell the future through a person's month of birth. Psychics say people have signs they are to live by, eliminating the need for God. This was something that I lived by when I was living in a worldly lifestyle. I wouldn't even leave my house until I had read my horoscope. I wore a medallion that stood for my sign as a good luck piece. This was an idol in my life because I trusted in that more than I trusted in God.

Even religious statues are kept in an attempt to get closer to God through the item, and for the items to protect the owner, instead of God himself and the angels of heaven. This can be people's attempts to protect themselves.

Witchcraft candles are normally about twelve inches high and approximately four inches wide, are made of glass with the wax inside, and have potions built into them. Curses are placed on the candles, and the person is advised to burn the candle for so many days to bring the assigned curse to themselves or to others. The candles cover a variety of things that the people may want. One candle can be to control. Another candle can be for supposed good luck. Now, this does not mean that every candle that you see is evil. I am talking about a very specific candle. Witchcraft is built on deceiving the people. People may want good luck, and maybe the candle that the witch has given them is really a candle for destruction—the opposite of what the person was trying to achieve. When I got involved in witchcraft, I told a person who was a warlock that I was having bad luck. The warlock told me he had just the thing to help me. Little did I know that the candle he gave me and the potions I was to apply for a week were for total mind control, chaos, and confusion!

The warlock was eventually saved. He gave his heart to Christ and went through days of deliverance, and then he came to me to apologize for what he had done to me by getting me involved in witchcraft. He had told me that it was white witchcraft and not evil at all, and I'd believed him. When he repented to me for what he had done, he said, "I lied to you. There is no such thing as white witchcraft or good witchcraft—it is all black and evil." This was my boyfriend at the time, and honestly I was very naive and had believed all the lies at the time.

After he got saved, he led me to Christ. He didn't know any scripture yet but shared with me how he'd met Christ, got saved, and been delivered through a deliverance ministry. Then he set up an appointment for me to be delivered as well. We had a long way to go to be set free; it was a step-by-step journey. I say that because there were things I learned through the deliverance ministry, but there were also things that I had to learn straight from God while walking hand in hand with my Lord and Savior Jesus Christ, who revealed every little, intricate thing that I had to know to not only be set free but stay free—and to keep my boyfriend, who would later become my husband, free.

About three years into my walk with the Lord, I was telling God that I wanted to get closer to him. He said to me, "Do you really want to get closer to me?"

I said, "Yes, Lord, of course I do."

He said again, "Do you really want to get closer to me?"

I said yes again. This went on over and over again. I finally said, "Why do you keep saying the same thing over and over?"

He said to me, "It will cost you something."

I said, "Yes, Lord. I know it will cost something."

The Lord replied, "You don't understand. It will cost you in getting rid of some material items that are not of me that are in your life." He started to teach me about graven images, statues, and other items that were separating me from a closer walk with him. He told me that I could still have a walk with him, but it would not be as intense as it would be with these things removed from my life. He showed me scriptures.

I questioned some things at first because some items had cost me a lot of money, and I didn't want to throw them away. I quickly learned that if God was telling me to get rid of something, then once I did, there would be blessings around the corner for being obedient in doing what the

Lord was asking me to do. He replaced everything that I had to get rid of with much better things. I have never been sorry for anything I have done for the Lord in obedience to him. It is fulfilling and rewarding when you place your trust in him!

House Anointing

But in a great house there are not only vessels of gold
and of silver, but also of wood and of earth; and some
to honor; and some to dishonor.
—2 Timothy 2:20

I understand that this scripture is used to explain purging yourself of
things that are not unto honor. I also see this scripture to literally mean
your physical house. The house that you live in needs to be purged! If
what you own is demonic in nature, it sends a statement to the demons
that you are still attached to them. At times I am called to do a house
anointing. The person asking for the house anointing may simply want
the anointing of God on their home, but there are many times that the
people who are requesting the house anointing are really asking because
they feel that the home is haunted. I have known people who are having
pictures falling off of walls, doors opening and closing, and footsteps
that they hear when no one is there. At times they may see spirits in
the house. They may be tormented in their own homes. Or it may be
something much more simple, like the fact that they cannot pray or
read in their home without feeling distracted, or they feel oppressed,
or a sense of heaviness is in their home.

There are a variety of reasons for this, and a house anointing is a good
place to start in revealing what the real problem is. To anoint the home,
I go into every room and do the sign of the cross with the anointing

oil, and I consecrate the home holy unto God. Then I bind up every spirit off of the home in each room, and I break any curses done in the house. Sometimes it is revealed to me that the curse was done through a previous owner. I then pray for God to reveal anything to me that is not holy and of God, as well as anything demonic that needs to be exposed. The items that we acquire in life can be to honor or to dishonor. America is a melting pot for every nationality—and for many varieties of witchcraft. Every nationality has its own superstitions or its own forms of witchcrafts. Also, we live in the world, and many people do not realize that some things that we can buy in a store can be a gateway to the demonic if we are not aware of what is holy and what is not holy.

I have found through my experience of doing deliverances for over thirty years that the deliverance will go smoother if the people who are being delivered have cleaned out their homes of demonic items. If our entertainment is from demons, it is like saying that we believe in them, like them, and give them the right to be in our lives. Having demonic items in our homes gives the devil and his demons the right to enter!

For example, some items would be things with demon pictures on them, statues of demons, statues of dragons, and pentagrams (the five-sided star inside of a circle). You know the simple peace sign with a circle, a line running down the middle, and two legs coming out from the middle? If you turn that symbol around, you will find that it is an upside down cross with the two legs broken! These are just a few items. Ouija boards are board games in which people use spirits to move an object around a board to answer questions and give them their future. They ask the board questions, and the pointer moves through spirit power to each individual letter to spell out the answer. Each board has curses and evil spirits assigned to it. When the person plays the game, the demon spirits attach to the person and stay in that person's life until the curse and the demons are renounced and cast out of their lives. Eight balls are another game that works in the same way of foretelling the future, where the person playing the game asks questions, and the eight ball answers yes or no. This also has spirits attached to it.

Crystals are another demonic item and are used for the point at the top of the crystal as the focal point of power for the demons to enter. This is a portal of power for the demonic. The crystals are used in New Age, which is a form of witchcraft. People involved in New Age worship the moon, the sun, and the stars. They may have statues of the sun, moon, and stars, and some statues have faces painted or engraved on them to make them look alive. Dream catchers are another item where the demons can come through the web located in the center. These dream catchers have spirits attached to them. Many people have bought these items because they have a problem sleeping, and they are told that this dream catcher will help them to sleep better—only to find out that now they are being tormented and cannot sleep at all because now an evil spirit has entered into their bedroom and into their lives! Dream catchers normally have a circle and strings woven in the middle that look like a web, with feathers outlining the circle and hanging off of it. The spirits attached to this can cause havoc in the person's life. The circle is the portal of spirit power—an entrance for demons. Wind chimes were made so that the person could hear when the demonic spirits would come. As the chimes made noise, the person would know that the spirit had arrived.

We were called to a person's home who was having accidents all the time and was being tormented. This lady asked us to come to her home to anoint it. A couple weeks prior to her asking us to come over, she had an accident with her car right in front of my house. I heard a loud crash and felt a shaking. I ran to the window to see what had happened and saw a car flipped over. I ran out of the house to the car, where I saw a woman upside down in her car. She was very upset. Then I realized that I recognized her! I called 911 and helped her to get out of the car. She said that she was okay and then was taken by ambulance to the hospital.

Not too long after this episode, she called us to come over to her home. We arrived at her house and went room by room, placing the anointing oil in the sign of the cross in each and every room in the name of Jesus. We broke the curses off the home but didn't see anything that was unholy; this person had been a Christian for a very long time and for the most part was aware of what was not of God.

At the end of the anointing, the lady asked us, "Did you see anything that was not holy in my home?" I was just about ready to say no when I looked up in her basement. Up on a little window ledge in her basement was a statue. We pulled down the statue, and it was a Buddha statue. Underneath this statue was a prayer to the spirits of darkness.

The Word of God clearly states, "Thou shalt have no other gods before me" (Exodus 20:3).

The Buddha is another god. We quickly said, "Here it is! Here is what is causing all this havoc in your life! This is the problem right here!" She repented to God for having the evil item in her home, and she destroyed the statue and has not had any problems since. This was a quick remedy, but sometimes it is not as simple because there are some people who may have many, many demonic things displayed in their house; then it has to be a step-by-step process.

> And many that believed came, and confessed, and showed their deeds. Many of them also which used curious arts brought their books together, and burned them before all men: and they counted the price of them, and they found it fifty thousand pieces of silver. So mightily grew the word of God and prevailed. (Acts 19:18–20)

In the *Vines Expository Dictionary, arts* is explained as curious or magical arts.

This scripture in Acts 19 declares that the people first believed and then confessed, showed their deeds, and burned or destroyed their objects that were not of God. The amount was fifty thousand pieces of silver! This is a huge amount of money that had been spent on these items, and in the end they destroyed them! What I always say is, "How much is it worth for you to have peace in your life?" Jesus said to consider the cost! Though many of these things may cost a lot of money, if they are demonic, they will take away our peace in our lives and in our homes. My personal opinion is that material items are just that. They are only material, and the benefits of being set free through releasing these items, which are demonic, are endless! I have learned that whatever you release and give up or get rid of for God, he will replace it with far greater riches in his kingdom.

Now, when I say riches, I do not mean just money! Riches can also mean peace, success, healing, and deliverance. Whenever I do a deliverance, I always ask the person one thing, "If you could ask for one thing in your life that you would want God to do for you, what would that one thing be?" Almost always the answer is, "I would want peace!" Peace is more priceless than money to a person who is being tormented day and night.

In verse 20, the scripture says that in the end, after they destroyed their evil objects, the word of God grew! There is an anointing that comes to the person who gets rid of those unholy things for God. It pleases God when his children are willing to let go of those things that that had cost them money or had sentimental value but were ungodly, so that they can be cleansed and ultimately get closer to God by being obedient.

Horoscopes are another form of witchcraft in foretelling the future. These are designed by fortunetellers or witches who foretell the person's future through demonic spirits. When I had been involved in the occult, every day I looked at my horoscope. I would not even leave my house until I had read the horoscopes. I would burn incense and did prayers or curses over my crystals for my point of power. I trusted them to tell me how my day would go. I didn't trust God to tell me. I trusted in the horoscope (or the demons that they represented), which is given by psychics or witches, to direct my life and my path! After I was saved, I had to destroy these objects, repent, and renounce them and the demons that entered my life through these attachments.

The Lord has his people strategically placed in areas of influence, and this is also true of the devil. He has his people strategically placed in areas of our lives to draw us into his web of the occult. Nowadays, it is not uncommon to see witchcraft candles in a regular grocery store. You can buy candles that have curses placed in the wax, and you can buy them in a witchcraft shop. So be aware! What seems to be totally harmless is not always true. They may have many different varieties of curses on them. Some can have curses of control. Some can have curses of bondage on them. Some can even have curses of death. These candles can be revealed as demonic by the icons that are on the glass. They may have demonic pictures, or they may have religious pictures on them of saints and Mother Mary. Remember, the whole idea of the occult is deception. They work on deception, hoping that you will not know and will use it and get involved in it! My husband was involved in witchcraft, and he had pictures of Jesus and Mother Mary, different saints' pictures, statues of Mary and Jesus, and many other saint statues. This is not unusual.

Another item that has become popular is demon action figure toys. Some of them are based off of horror movies. Some of the names of these series are The Crow, Puppet Master, Axis of Evil, The Walking Dead, Five Nights at Freddy's, The Ghost, Spawn, Snowman, The Preacher (which is a mockery of preachers and has a demonic edge to it), werewolves and vampires sagas, Roué of the Dragon, and Congregation of Darkness. The manufacturers are Full Moon, McFarlane, The Crow, and more.

A young man who came to us had been saving these items as collector items. He had huge boxes of these toys, and many come with fake knives dipped in blood or with heads cut off. They are meant to look gruesome and scary. This man came to us because he was being tormented, was in total confusion, and could not finish sentences. He was not eating or sleeping. I knew we did not have much time to straighten this man out and bring some sanity to his life. Many things were done for him as far as ministering to him, but the big impact for him was getting rid of the demonic toys. A huge difference started to happen for this young man. People at his workplace noticed that he changed, and they asked him what he was doing that made this much of a difference. His boss noticed the change and allowed him to take off for a week with vacation pay so that he could spend more time with us and be ministered to. He is doing so much better now.

At one point when he first came to us, he said that in the back of his mind, he wanted to kill himself. He was slowly taking care of himself less and less, hoping that he would die. He was at the end of his rope and couldn't stop crying. He was in total despair, but now he now has hope. He is eating and said that he is sleeping better than he ever has slept in his life. Therefore I know that God has done a mighty miracle for this man.

Scary movies and horror movies are also something that need to be removed from the house.

> For God has not given us the spirit of fear. (2 Timothy 1:7)

God calls it a spirit. When we are watching things that have to do with fear, we are bringing in a spirit of fear.

> Fear hath torment. (1 John 4:18)

Many of these movies have to do with demons, evil spirits, haunted houses, mental telepathy, death, killing, horror, and fear. They induce fear, and many cannot sleep after seeing movies about gory death and eerie scenes. This is what so many raise their children on. God says he has not given the spirit of fear, because this fear will grow into torment! I have seen people so riddled with fear that they cannot speak, or they start to speak and cannot finish sentences, or they shake uncontrollably. I have seen people who have so much fear that it is affecting their health. They are having problems with their hearts, some to the point of having heart attacks. People can come down with serious diseases because we were never designed to live in fear, and we were never designed to be startled or shocked in horror on a regular basis. A healthy fear was designed to save us from dangerous situations. Our hearts cannot handle fear like what people receive from horror pictures, or from Halloween nights like fright night, where things jump out from around corners.

> Finally, my brethren, whatsoever things are true, whatsoever things are honest, whatsoever things are just, whatsoever things are pure, whatsoever things are lovely, whatsoever things are of a good report; if there be any virtue, and if there be any praise, think on these things. (Philippians 4:8)

This is the basis that I judge things on, regarding whether it is good or bad.

For heavy metal rock albums, look to see if it is talking about death, destruction, and killing. This is a good clue as to whether you need to get rid of something. Look to see if it is about darkness or gloom, or heaviness and despair and depression. What we feed our ears and what we feed our eyes is what will come into our lives, and spirits are allowed to enter in through the open doors that we have give to them.

I also learned that not only do you as a Christian need to be clean, but also your house needs to be clean. I started to clean out my house. I prayed every day, and I asked the Holy Spirit to lead me. Step by step, he showed me every object that was not of him that was in my home. And step by step, I felt more and more that anything demonic had to go. For me, I had to get rid of the crystals that I'd used in New Age, with the point of the crystal being the focal point of power for the demons to come through. These crystals often come with a prayer (which is really a curse attached to the crystal) that the person is to recite to bring up the spirits. Incense, which I would burn when calling up spirits, had to go.

Demonic music was also something we had to look at. My husband was into heavy metal and thrash. Mega Death, Black Sabbath, Marilyn Manson, Insane Clown Posse, Grateful Dead, Alice Cooper, King Crimson, Godsmack, and AC/DC are all based on the demonic. Thrash is another central theme of heavy metal, obsessed with chaos and involving mental illness, confusion, war, and hell demons. Bands go at this theme to find excitement within it for deep personal and emotional involvement. Sometimes it can be the band reflecting on the human condition through their music. The prime reason for its controversy is anti-Christian, and it shows scenes like Satan, hell, and evil. Some bands actually killed animals on stage as a sacrifice; this was called speed metal. These forms of music are created to usher in the demonic and to usher in Satanism and various forms of witchcraft.

Books and teaching materials dealing with the arts of Satanism, sorcery, spiritism, voodoo, atheism, false doctrine, false religions, and cults need to be cleaned out of the home.

Some of the Disney movies and toys are based on witchcraft. One of the first times we see Mickey Mouse, he is shown with the hat that goes to a point with the moon and star symbols. The tall blue hat with the point is the point of power for the demonic. Many of the stories have a witch in them. Remember that witches fly on broomsticks, and the broomsticks stand for astral projection. This is done by the power of the demonic. In some of the stories, the characters fly. They are flying through the power of witchcraft. Remember that it is called the Magic Kingdom. Peter Pan flies through the air through astral projection, which is witchcraft. Cinderella has witchcraft in it. Cinderella is visited by the good fairy. However, fairies are a form of demon. Her coach is changed into a pumpkin; the rats are what pull the coach. Aladdin has a genie friend, and genies are a nice name for demons. A witch enchanted Snow White. *Into the Woods* is magical thinking and is about death and destruction. The movie *Maleficent* has the main character, who is in all black, look like a demon, and she has the horns of Satan on her. *Beauty and the Beast* is our first introduction to bestiality for children! Tinker Bell is a fairy with a magic scepter!

These things are meant to train up our children into witchcraft and desensitize them, thought maybe not purposefully by the people creating it. But Satan does plan for these things to introduce them to the supernatural. That way, when witchcraft is introduced to them, they think it is fun, harmless, and not real. They are desensitized to the point that if someone tells them how to do out-of-body experiences, to them it is not bad because they have seen it in cartoons and children's movies. Therefore it must be harmless.

I want to warn every person out there that this is not harmless. The devil promises power as HIS subjects delve into more of the occult. But there is a point where the devil is done with that person, turns on them, and pulls the rug out from under them. then they do not know what to do to get set free. *Bewitched* was about a witch, and the grandmother was a witch. Then there was *Sabrina the Teenage Witch*, who has two aunts who are witches and a black cat!

Crystal balls are used to foretell the future. Four-leaf clovers are for good luck, and luck is based on spirits, not on God's blessing. There is a huge difference between the two concepts. Tarot cards are also witchcraft. A lot of games have witchcraft in them. Some of the games actually have curses involved in them. You go through the different levels to obtain the new demons. They don't call them that, but that is what they are. Dungeons and Dragons, Warcraft, and Harry Potter have witchcraft in them. Wrath of Demons, Journey, Pathfinder Battles, Demons versus Wizards, Perfect World International—all are demonic games. Some are obvious from their names and some are not. Halloween items such as witches, warlocks, gremlins, demons, imps, dwarves, Dracula, black spiders, black cats, and pumpkins with faces on them stand for the spirits inside. Also, the masks with the cutouts stand for demon spirits behind the mask. Marti Gras masks come from the holiday called carnival and are from medieval England, introduced to America in the 1600s.

> Take ye good heed unto yourselves; for ye saw no manner of similitude on the day that the Lord spake unto you in Horeb out of the midst of the fire: Lest ye corrupt yourselves, and make you a graven image, the similitude of any figure, the likeness of male or female, The likeness of any beast that is on the earth, the likeness of any winged fowl that flieth in the air, The likeness of any thing that creepeth on the ground, the likeness of any fish that is in the waters beneath the earth: And lest thou lift up thine eyes unto heaven, and when thou seest the sun, and the moon, and the stars, even all the host of heaven, shouldest be driven to worship them, and serve them, which the Lord thy God has divided unto all the nations under the whole heaven. (Deuteronomy 4:15–19)

Here in Deuteronomy, God gives a clear explanation of things we are not to make into statues and graven images. Verse 19 tells us that we can be driven to worship them instead of the creator!

Take heed unto yourselves, lest you forget the covenant of the Lord thy God, which he made with you, and make you a graven image, or the likeness of anything, which the Lord thy God hath forbidden you. (Deuteronomy 4:23)

For there is one God, and one mediator between God and men, the man Christ Jesus; Who gave himself for a ransom for all, to be testified in due time. (1 Timothy 2:5–6)

This tells me that Jesus is the *only* one whom we can go through as our mediator to get to God. Not Mary, not St. Christopher, and not any other dead saint. Not Buddha, not Allah, and not the pope! Not to a medal with a saint on it. We cannot get closer to God through a statue, but only through Jesus Christ! We do not need to have good luck pieces to help our lives go right. We do not have to trust in luck; we now can trust in the power of the living God. We can now fully put our trust in God for what we need. We do not need statues of angels, or of Jesus as a statue on the cross. Our victory is in the empty cross. He defeated death, hell, and the grave. He is no longer on the cross but has risen from the dead!

Divination, Soothsaying, Enchanters, Sorcery, Charmers, Familiar Spirits, and Necromancy

When thou art come into the land which the LORD thy God giveth thee, thou shalt not learn to do after the abominations of those nations. There shall not be found among you any one that maketh his son or his daughter to pass through the fire, or that useth divination, or an observer of times, or an enchanter, or a witch. Or a charmer, or a consulter with familiar spirits, or a wizard, or a necromancer. For all that do these things are an abomination unto the Lord: and because of these abominations the LORD thy God doeth drive them out from before thee. Thou shalt be perfect with the Lord thy God. For these nations, which thou shalt possess, hearkened unto observers of times, and unto diviners: but as for thee, the Lord thy God has not suffered thee to do so.
—Deuteronomy 18:9–14

These are all arts of the demonic realm. We are not to do them, dabble in them, or have anything related to them, such as material items that are used in various practices of the occult! Necromancy is something that not too many people know about. Necromancy is the art of speaking to the dead, and it is forbidden by God. Speaking to dead saints such as St. Christopher, St. Mary, or St. Andrew is necromancy.

Trusting in medals with dead saints on them is forbidden by God. Medals of St. Mary are something that people use as a good luck medal or an avenue of protection. Jesus, God the Father, the Holy Spirit, and our angels are our protection. The Hail Mary prayer is a prayer that the person does to give honor to Mary instead of Jesus Christ. Our only mediator from us to God is Jesus Christ. We shouldn't have these items that open a door to the demonic, and we shouldn't involve ourselves in these practices. It opens the door to familiar spirits. Familiar spirits, or familial spirits, are spirits that take on the appearance of those who have died and appear to us. Because they are something we are familiar with, the demons know that we will more easily accept them into our lives. The demons then enter into our lives and can possess that person. It is time to close the door and destroy the graven images, idols, and statues. Throw them away and renounce the practices of giving honor to demonic ceremonies. Many will pray to these spirits and talk to them because they come to them as someone they know. This is an abomination.

The demonic can be displayed in a variety of forms. If the person has been involved in the occult, or someone who previously lived in the home was involved in the occult, curses most likely have been placed on that home. There are curses of Satanism, witchcraft, sorcery, spiritism, black magic, voodoo, and Santeria, just to name a few!

> But if I cast out devils by the Spirit of God, then the kingdom of God is come unto you. Or else how can one enter into a strong man's house, and spoil his goods, except he first bind the strong man? and then he will spoil his house. (Matthew 12:28–29)

Jesus is clearly speaking about deliverance. He explains that in deliverance, he gives us a key to be successful in the deliverance, and the key is that you bind up the strongman. There is a main spirit over that person who is over all the other spirits that are on them. If you bind up that strongman, the others are weakened and brought to confusion, and then Jesus explains that you will spoil that house and defeat it!

Whatever the type of witchcraft the person has been involved in, it is the strongman who has to be bound before even starting the deliverance. If the person was involved in witchcraft, the strongman of witchcraft has to be bound up before casting the other spirits out of the person. It could also be a strong man of religion, voodoo, or control.

Many times if a person has been deeply involved in the occult, there will be what I call a nest. Usually this is placed on the headboard of the person's bed; at other times, it can be over a main doorway. This needs to be removed and destroyed to be on the safe side. Wear gloves, because many are covered in potions or oils. Also, there can be altars in the home if the person is deeply involved in the various forms of witchcraft. This altar is where the person who is involved in the occult meets with the demons and even does sacrifices or curses.

It is helpful to know what has been done in the house concerning the occult, so that all demonic activity can be broken and cleansed by the blood of Jesus Christ and the demons can be expelled out of the home and ultimately out of their lives. If I do a deliverance on people, but they go back into their houses where all there witchcraft items are, then they can come back into their lives. I like to see that this has been done already and that all practices are renounced.

One man who came to me was involved in Satanism for most of his life. He was very mixed up and tormented. He didn't trust too many people, and the trust that he did have was minimal. He came to our church over a space of two years. He would pop in on prayer night, tell some of his problems, and be in a hurry to go because he had to go to work. He would stop in one night, and then we wouldn't see him for weeks or even months. But we continued to pray for him to come back and to learn to trust us. We prayed for him to have more time to speak to us so that he wouldn't be in such a hurry; this would give us the opportunity to minister to him.

Finally, one night he showed up, and everything was beginning to crumble around him. He came with so much more sincerity. He then explained that his life was crumbling around him, and he needed help. He was willing to surrender to the Lordship of Jesus Christ. He said he would do whatever I asked him to do, if I would deliver him and set him free.

I was glad but also knew that he was in a very weakened state. I knew that he had never known anything but darkness, and so I came to the conclusion that this was going to be something that would take a great amount of time and patience. I explained to him that this was not an instant fix, and off he would go. I told him that this would be step by step procedure. I told him that we would start by anointing his house. As we walked through the front door, I noticed the house was very dark. He had paintings that he had painted all over the walls. He was a beautifully gifted artist, but I noticed something else: all of his paintings were about depression and people crying, and there were pictures of the flames of hell, death, and destruction. One painting was an abstract of different colors, and as I looked closer, I could see a demon's face in the picture. I knew what he was painting was coming from what was inside his heart. Although I knew these paintings had to go, I also knew that there was something much worse as a root in this house and in his life.

We went anointing through the house. When we got to the upstairs, there was one room where I could feel the eeriness emanating from the room even before I stepped into it. When I went to grab the door knob, a big gush of wind hit me, and I was thrown back. My ladies who were behind me grabbed me so that I wouldn't fall over. I was being hit by the forces that wanted to stop me from going into that room. I then said, "In the name of Jesus, I bind up every spirit of darkness, and I command them to back off in Jesus's name. I disarm you before Almighty God, and I will come into this room and cast you out!" I then was able to open the door and step in.

There were huge, plastic storage bins in this room that were six feet long, and there was about ten of them. Inside of them were demonic action toys he had saved all of his life, still in the packages. But they were total gore! Heads cut off, fake blood dripping down, ghost action toys, goblins, and even a demonic preacher. I could understand why he was going through so much. He had boxes of magazines that were all about the demonic. These were supposed to be children's magazines, but really they were all about death, destruction, and murder. I knew these things had to go, but I also knew that there was so much stuff to destroy that it was going to be a huge job. I had never seen this amount of demonic items in my whole time as a Christian. We started with the room that was the worst upstairs. We got paper shredders, and I put shifts of different people to the task of getting rid of the items.

At first this man was not much help because he was going through tremendous attacks in his mind from the demons who did not want this deliverance to happen. As we gradually cleaned out the house, we ministered to him and finally were able to get to know him and his story of what had happened to him. He said at first that he didn't feel anything happening. I told him that was okay. It was like peeling layers of the demonic off of him. He was involved in so many things in his life that was demonic, and this would take a little while to change. I also stated to him that he never knew anything normal, and so it took over fifty years of satanic involvement to mess his life up He needed to give God the time to change his life back to normal.

We proceeded to get rid of the demonic items, and after the first week, he started to notice a change. By the third week, he finally took a week off from work so that we would have more than one or two days to work on his home. Other workers noticed the change. One employee, whom he'd hated and wanted to fight for years, went up to him and asked for forgiveness. He told me that this man was so shocked at the change in him, and he bought him a drink as a peace offering between them. I was so pleased. The ministering about forgiving, repenting, and unforgiveness was working.

He had been abused as a child by his mother, and I explained that he needed to forgive her. This forgiveness would not only help set her free but also set him free as well. He did so, and he spoke with his mother. Healing started to take place on that front. Years and years of hatred, anger, and frustration were finally being healed. In the third week, I noticed that even the sound of his voice had changed. I was so amazed at what God was doing. All glory goes to God! We ministered to him about so many things in his life, and step by step the torment left. The demonic things left his home. The pictures were destroyed last, and he decided to do that one. I told him that every time he destroyed the pictures of depression and death, he was making a statement to the devil that he no longer wanted him in his life.

Since then, he has renounced Satanism and witchcraft, and he has been involved in the cleansing of unholy feelings and unholy relationships. He has undergone healing in his heart. I am still involved with him to this point, but I know now we are coming through the home stretch for him. He was an alcoholic when we first met with him, but now he told me that the temptation of it was almost totally gone from his life. He was very shocked that the strong feelings about drinking were drifting away. We were patient because I knew that the amount of evil things in his home were in the thousands, leaving an open door. Piece by piece it was being cleansed out, and I also knew that there were many demons attacking this man. I had him renounce the drinking and delivered him from the alcoholism, but there were times he fell. I understood that it was going to take time, and I would not give up on him. He was so grateful that I didn't give up! He would cry almost every time we met with him. He was so full of remorse for what he had done in his life, but I saw in him that God was going to use him in a mighty way once he was totally set free, and once he learned and grew in Christianity.

If a person has gone to many types of witches (sometimes in an attempt to get set free by a different form of witchcraft), she starts to have layers of different types of witchcraft, and each type will have its own guard dogs around the spirits. Guard dog spirits are just what they sound like: they have been placed around the main spirit to protect it. They are usually something like a gargoyle or pit bull, or it can be named after a spirit from Africa, or Haiti if the witches are into Voodoo. No matter the names of the spirits, you need to make sure you are fasting and praying so that you can seek God before the deliverance and allow him to reveal what you are fighting.

It is good practice to bind up the guard dogs and cast them out, in order to go on to the next spirit. Now the other individual spirits will have much less strength. This will make deliverance so much easier and more effective!

I will list the definitions of various types of witchcraft. Many people talk about different witchcrafts, and they mention different names of witches. If we know these names, and someone conveys to you what they have been involved with, you will know what has to be cast out of them.

There are many different types of witchcraft. Not everyone calls herself a witch, and there is a lot of variety, even among people who follow the same path. The following is a general list of different religions related to witchcraft. There may be others, but this is will give you an idea of the various types. Some of these vary greatly from Wicca, but they are related in one form or another.

> Witchcraft, Wicca, Witta, Pagan, Neo-pagan, Ceremonial Magick, Kemetic, Tameran, Discordian, Erisian, Chaos Magician, Gardnerian, Alexandrian, Reclaiming, Dianic, Norse, Asatru, Odinism, Shamanism, Hindu, Huna, Mama Chi Native, Indiginous, Druid, Earth Religion, The Craft, Old Religion, Voodoo, Vodun, Santeria, Yoruba, Golden Dawn, Circle, Yoruba, Bruja, Cunandero, Silva Mind, Recon, Reconstructionist, Kitchen Witch, New Age, Soothsayer, Enchanter, Goth, Divination, Sorcery, Charmer, Necromancy

Here is a list of different types of witches.

> Augery Witch, Ceremonial Witch, Eclectic Witch, Fiery Witch, Green Witch, Hedge Witch, Heredity Witch, Kitchen Witch, Solitary Witch, Satanic Witch, Warlock

A head witch is involved in all of these witchcrafts and has mastered all of the various types.

All of these things are forbidden by God in Deuteronomy 18:9–14, and if we have been involved in any type of witchcraft, we need to repent of it and be set free. It is an abomination before God.

A Few Last Thoughts

As I am writing this last chapter of my book, I am thinking about all the things that have transpired in America over the last few years. So much has changed in our country. These are troubling times that we are living in right now for our country, for our churches, and for the Christian believer. Over the past thirty years, I have seen so much of Christianity be systematically taken out of society. We are now being inundated with so much evil. Everywhere you look, evil is being pushed on us. God has been taken out of society step by step over the years. Now we see witchcraft out in the open—it is not even being hidden anymore.

The division in our country is at a level that I have never seen before. It is no longer gray but instead it is purely black and white. We have seen God taken out of every area of our country, and now we are seeing the fruits of it in our everyday lives. There are mass shootings in movie theatres, mass shootings in elementary schools, and mass shootings in church, the one place we never thought we would see it.

In these last days—which I do feel that we are in right now—the Church needs to be prepared! We need to pray as never before. We need to be prepared for the influx of people that are going to come into the Church not just to visit but to be set free. The Church needs to be ready and able to deliver those who have no hope left. The Church needs to be prepared to handle those who have given their lives over to the dark side, only to find that it has led them to total emptiness and left them in dire distress. We are their only hope. The Church is the only entity out there that can help these people who are entangled in a web that they cannot get out of.

The Lord has told me that deliverance churches are going to need more people in their deliverance teams to handle this influx that will surely come into their sanctuaries. In the end, the one thing I know about the devil is that he always turns on his own people when he is through with them. He pulls the rug out from under them, and they will be looking for help. My prayer is that the Church will be ready, willing, and able to handle these people. I have had people come to me and say, "You are my last hope!" I have had people say to me that if I didn't help them right then, they were going home to kill themselves. We have the answer to their emptiness, and it is Jesus Christ and his power to deliver them.

A person said to me the other day that she really didn't feel called to doing deliverance or spiritual warfare. I will close with this reply,

> And these signs shall follow them that believe; in my name shall they cast out devils; they shall speak with new tongues; They shall take up serpents; and if they drink any deadly thing, it shall not hurt them; they shall lay hands on the sick, and they shall recover. (Mark 16:17–18)

Jesus himself told us that these signs shall follow those who believe! If Jesus himself said it, then it is good enough for me. He promises us that we will be able to do the things that he did when we received him into our hearts and into our lives. His spirit lives inside of us. It is his power working through us to do the supernatural and achieve the victory!

About the Author

Judith Garcia is an Ordained Pastor in Rochester New York. Judith is Senior Pastor of her church. She has been doing deliverances since the early 1980's Her church specializes in healing, deliverance, and spiritual warfare. She was involved in the occult at a young age, and went through a deliverance ministry where she came to know Jesus Christ as her Lord and Savior and ultimately was set free from the powers of darkness. Along with her husband who was preparing to become High Priest in Witchcraft, but instead, gave his life over to God through the same deliverance ministry.

This book is a compilation of her knowledge that she has learned through the years of hands on experience and knowledge of setting the captives free! Judith shares through her writings, the steps and stages, and the onward progression that she learned through her walk with God, and through her ministry to set others free from the shackles of darkness.

Judith has made a commitment for the advancing of the Kingdom of God, by setting those free who have found themselves entangled in a life of the occult! Showing people the love of Christ Jesus to transform their lives to be mighty, powerful soldiers of the Kingdom of God!

Printed in the United States
By Bookmasters